101 BRIDGE MAXIMS

by H. W. Kelsey

THE BRIDGE WORLD
39 WEST 94th STREET
NEW YORK, N. Y. 10025

Published by
Devyn Press
Louisville, Kentucky

Cover by Bonnie Baron Pollack

Printed in the United States of America.

Devyn Press
151 Thierman Lane
Louisville, KY 40207

ISBN 0-910791-10-4

TABLE OF CONTENTS

INTRODUCTION

Many bridge players, resigned to the fact that they are no longer making real progress at the game, have settled into a predictable sort of rut. Year after year they commit the same old mistakes, conceding their 800's, doubling opponents into game, missing laydown slams, and going down in contracts that they suspect they should be making. These players would like to play a better game but are not prepared to put much effort into the process of learning. And quite right, too. Bridge is meant to be enjoyed, and much of the fun is lost if one has to spend long hours agonizing over complicated rules of bidding and play.

And yet there is a simple way of bringing about a solid improvement. The application of a number of easy-to-learn principles is all that is needed to save vast amounts of money or match points over the course of a year. These principles or maxims are etched deep in the memory of every good player, and they will be vaguely familiar to every player who has passed beyond the beginner stage. The trouble is that, while accepting the maxim and admitting its validity, players have difficulty in recalling it at the right time — during the play of the hand to which it applies.

There is a problem of recognition here. It is only when a player is truly familiar with a hazard, either from his own experience or from extensive reading, that he is able to say: 'Ah, yes. I know the maxim that applies here.' It is this failure in diagnosis that leads players to make the same mistakes over and over again.

A maxim may be defined as a general truth drawn from experience. Profiting from the experience of others is one of the short-cuts to success in any field, and the brief, stylized form of the maxim makes it easy to absorb and remember.

There would be little point in setting out principles without example hands. The best lesson hands illustrate points that apply not only to those particular deals but to a whole group of related deals. From a portfolio of well-chosen hands it is possible to mine priceless nuggets of general information.

Each maxim in this book represents the kernel of wisdom and truth extracted from the deal that accompanies it. Most of the hands can be placed at intermediate level but, as befits a book published close to 1984, some are more intermediate than others. The deals covers the entire spectrum of bridge skills — bidding, leading, signaling, defending and playing the hand — and they are arranged in no particular order. There may be some overlapping in places, and certain of the maxims might more properly be described as miscellaneous hints or tips. I trust that none is truly redundant.

A word of warning may be necessary. Do not take any maxim too seriously, for slogans should never be allowed to degenerate into parrot cries. A maxim such as 'Never take an unnecessary finesse' may hold good in all circumstances: others will not have the same overall validity. Look out always for the exception that proves the rule, and remember that flexibility is the most priceless asset at the bridge table.

I am confident that the application of the maxims set out in this book will enable you to improve your game out of all recognition. After a single reading you will find yourself making contracts and producing defenses that would have seemed beyond you in the past.

Good luck!

1. NO BARGAIN

Many declarers have a natural urge to win tricks as cheaply as possible, but this is not always the right policy. This hand from a team game might have come straight from a manual on elementary play.

<pre>
              ♠ 6
              ♡ Q 10 3
              ◇ Q 7 4
              ♣ K Q 10 8 6 3
                   N
                W   E
                   S
              ♠ A K 9 3
              ♡ A 9 6
              ◇ A J 5 2
              ♣ J 4
</pre>

N-S vulnerable
Dealer South

SOUTH	WEST	NORTH	EAST
1 NT	Pass	3 NT	Pass
Pass	Pass		

At both tables South played in three notrump and received the lead of the five of hearts. The three was played from dummy, East produced the eight and at one table South won a cheap trick with the nine.

The jack of clubs was allowed to win the next trick. West took his ace of clubs on the second round and played the two of spades to the jack and king. Seeking a way into dummy, South tried the effect of leading the jack of diamonds but there were no takers. On the next round of diamonds East captured dummy's queen with the king and returned a heart, and South found himself unable to make more than seven tricks.

Avid readers of textbooks will of course have realized that South should have won the first trick with the ace of hearts in order to preserve a later entry in dummy for the long clubs. There is no danger in this course, for the Rule of Eleven indicates that the eight is East's only heart higher than the five.

The complete deal:

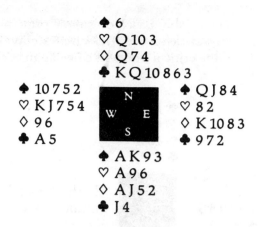

```
                    ♠ 6
                    ♡ Q 10 3
                    ◇ Q 7 4
                    ♣ K Q 10 8 6 3
    ♠ 10 7 5 2          N          ♠ Q J 8 4
    ♡ K J 7 5 4     W       E      ♡ 8 2
    ◇ 9 6               S          ◇ K 10 8 3
    ♣ A 5                          ♣ 9 7 2
                    ♠ A K 9 3
                    ♡ A 9 6
                    ◇ A J 5 2
                    ♣ J 4
```

At the other table South was not so greedy. He won the heart lead with the ace, knocked out the ace of clubs, won the spade switch and played another heart. West was unable to deny him access to dummy, and the declarer had ten tricks without needing to risk the diamond finesse.

MAXIM. Don't be miserly with your high cards. A cheap trick is no bargain if it denies you a later entry.

---

2. WHAT MATTERS IN DEFENSE

Good defense is invariably based on simple principles such as counting the number of defensive tricks that are available. On the following hand the critical moment came at an early stage in the play.

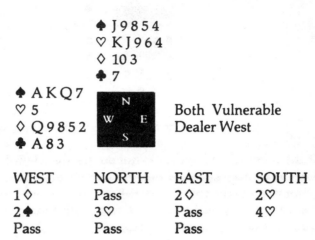

♠ J9854
♡ KJ964
◇ 103
♣ 7

♠ AKQ7
♡ 5
◇ Q9852
♣ A83

Both Vulnerable
Dealer West

WEST	NORTH	EAST	SOUTH
1◇	Pass	2◇	2♡
2♠	3♡	Pass	4♡
Pass	Pass	Pass	

West began with the ace of spades on which East played the six and South the three. Since the two of spades was missing, West could be fairly sure that he partner had started an echo to show a doubleton. He therefore cashed a second spade and wondered what to do next.

It made no difference what he did next, for his chance to defeat the contract had come and gone. The complete deal was as follows:

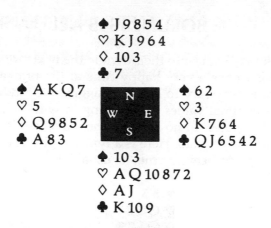

♠ J 9 8 5 4
♥ K J 9 6 4
♦ 10 3
♣ 7

♠ A K Q 7
♥ 5
♦ Q 9 8 5 2
♣ A 8 3

♠ 6 2
♥ 3
♦ K 7 6 4
♣ Q J 6 5 4 2

♠ 10 3
♥ A Q 10 8 7 2
♦ A J
♣ K 10 9

At trick three West switched, too late, to a diamond. South captured the king with his ace and used dummy's trump entries to ruff out the spades, establishing the fifth card in the suit for a discard of the jack of diamonds. Dummy still had two trumps left, and that was enough to take care of two of the club losers.

There was no need for West to help with the establishment of the spades in this way; his second spade trick could not disappear. He should have realized that two spades and a club trick would not be enough to defeat the contract. A diamond trick was required, and the right time to switch to diamonds is at trick two. The king forces out the ace, and the declarer cannot avoid the loss of two spades, one diamond and one club.

MAXIM. Establish tricks for your side, not for the opponents.

---

3. BOLDNESS IS ALL

The meek may come into their own in the next world but they certainly don't have a very happy time at the bridge table. To score well it is necessary to cultivate aggressive bidding habits, opening on minimal values and coming in with light overcalls and takeout doubles. In no form of the game is this more vital than at match-point pairs. Here is a typical episode from a pairs tournament where meekness met its usual fate.

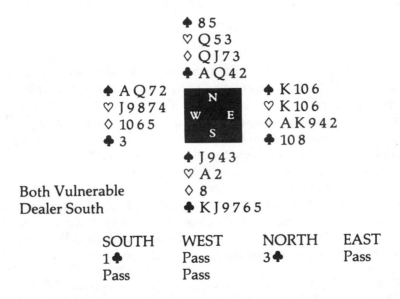

```
                    ♠ 8 5
                    ♡ Q 5 3
                    ◇ Q J 7 3
                    ♣ A Q 4 2
      ♠ A Q 7 2         N         ♠ K 10 6
      ♡ J 9 8 7 4    W     E      ♡ K 10 6
      ◇ 10 6 5          S         ◇ A K 9 4 2
      ♣ 3                          ♣ 10 8
                    ♠ J 9 4 3
                    ♡ A 2
                    ◇ 8
                    ♣ K J 9 7 6 5
```

Both Vulnerable
Dealer South

SOUTH	WEST	NORTH	EAST
1♣	Pass	3♣	Pass
Pass	Pass		

There were no more than four tricks to be lost, and South's score of 110 for making his contract of three clubs represented eighty per cent of the match points.

East and West can take at least nine tricks in hearts or diamonds, but it is not too easy for them to get into the auction after South's aggressive opening bid and North's double raise. Even so, a bold West might have ventured an overcall of one heart, while a thruster in the East would have doubled three clubs for takeout.

West had a further chance to contest when his opponents subsided at the three-level. His partner was then marked with substantial values, and West might have considered reopening with a bid of three hearts.

Three timid decisions in succession led to the inevitable result of a poor score.

MAXIM.   Get into the bidding whenever you can.

---

4. EXTRA CHANCE

Elimination play can increase the chances of success on many deals. This hand from a pairs tournament quickly sorted out the winners from the losers.

                     ♠ K J 7
                     ♡ A 9 4
                     ◊ A 10 3 2
                     ♣ 8 7 3

                     ♠ A 9 5 4
                     ♡ K Q J 7 6 3
Both Vulnerable   ◊ K 9 6
Dealer South   ♣ ——

SOUTH	WEST	NORTH	EAST
1♡	Pass	2◊	Pass
4♡	Pass	6♡	Pass
Pass	Pass		

The above sequence may be a little short of science, but most pairs managed to reach the small slam in hearts in one way or another.

After ruffing the opening lead of the ace of clubs, many declarers drew trumps in two rounds and continued with the ace, king, and another diamond. The suit proved to be 3-3, and on winning with the queen West returned another club for South to ruff. Since the remaining diamond in dummy could furnish only one spade discard, the declarers had to fall upon the spade finesse and the slam was defeated when East produced the queen.

Those who had some knowledge of end-play technique gave themselves an extra chance by eliminating the clubs before putting the opponents on lead. After ruffing the opening club lead they played the king and ace of hearts, ruffed a club, returned to dummy with the ace of diamonds and ruffed the last

club. The king and another diamond then put West on lead.
The full deal:

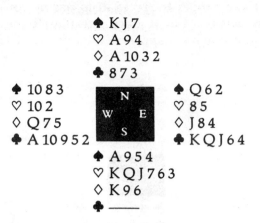

```
              ♠ K J 7
              ♡ A 9 4
              ◇ A 10 3 2
              ♣ 8 7 3
♠ 10 8 3                      ♠ Q 6 2
♡ 10 2           N           ♡ 8 5
◇ Q 7 5       W     E        ◇ J 8 4
♣ A 10 9 5 2     S           ♣ K Q J 6 4
              ♠ A 9 5 4
              ♡ K Q J 7 6 3
              ◇ K 9 6
              ♣ ———
```

In with the queen of diamonds, West had the choice of
conceding a ruff and discard or opening up the spades, and no
matter which course he adopted the slam rolled home. It would
have made no difference if West had unblocked the queen of
diamonds to allow East to win the trick.

MAXIM.   Give yourself an extra chance by removing the
defenders' exit cards before throwing them in.

---

5. CAUTIONARY TALE

It is right and proper to try to keep partner on the rails by signaling in defense, but it does not pay to be too heavy-handed. Look at what happened on this hand from a team game.

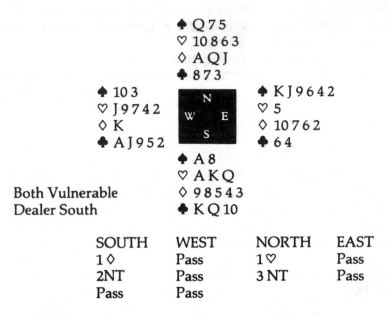

```
                    ♠ Q 7 5
                    ♡ 10 8 6 3
                    ◇ A Q J
                    ♣ 8 7 3
    ♠ 10 3                          ♠ K J 9 6 4 2
    ♡ J 9 7 4 2        N            ♡ 5
    ◇ K             W     E         ◇ 10 7 6 2
    ♣ A J 9 5 2        S            ♣ 6 4
                    ♠ A 8
                    ♡ A K Q
Both Vulnerable     ◇ 9 8 5 4 3
Dealer South        ♣ K Q 10
```

SOUTH	WEST	NORTH	EAST
1◇	Pass	1♡	Pass
2NT	Pass	3NT	Pass
Pass	Pass		

The bidding was the same in both rooms, and in one room the normal lead of the five of clubs was made. This ran to the ten and the declarer had no difficulty in racking up one spade, three hearts, four diamonds and two clubs for a total of ten tricks.

In the other room West found the only way to give the defense a chance when he led the ten of spades. East encouraged with the nine, telling his partner he had hit the jackpot but also telling the declarer how to play the hand.

South reasoned that since East appeared to have a good spade suit he could hardly have the ace of clubs, for he would then have made himself heard in the bidding. There was no point in winning the first trick in that case, so South held up his ace until the second round.

After cashing three rounds of diamonds (West discarding clubs) and three rounds of hearts, South played the ten of hearts, placing the lead firmly in the West hand. After cashing two hearts and the ace of clubs, West had to concede the last two tricks in clubs. The swing on the board was thus held to 1 IMP.

East's nine of spades at trick one was a complete giveaway. The play of the four or six, or even the jack, would have left open for South the possibility that West might have led away from the king of spades. South might then have ruined his chances by winning the first trick.

Having no outside entry, East should have seen the need to persuade South to take his ace of spades at once.

MAXIM.   **Signal with discretion.**

---

6. THE VAN WINKLE SYNDROME

It is all too easy to take a little nap when defending with poor cards. It can also be highly embarrassing, for the worst hand at the table may have a vital role to play in the defense. See what happened on this hand from a team-of-four match.

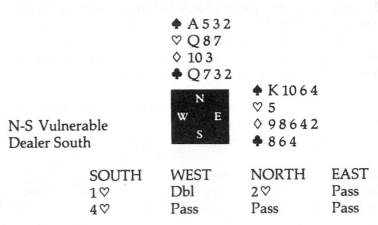

```
              ♠ A 5 3 2
              ♡ Q 8 7
              ◊ 10 3
              ♣ Q 7 3 2
                              ♠ K 10 6 4
                              ♡ 5
N-S Vulnerable                ◊ 9 8 6 4 2
Dealer South                  ♣ 8 6 4
```

SOUTH	WEST	NORTH	EAST
1♡	Dbl	2♡	Pass
4♡	Pass	Pass	Pass

The contract was the same in both rooms as was the opening lead of the queen of spades. A low card was played from dummy, and in one room East sleepily followed with the six of spades.

That was the end of the defense. East had no further opportunity to gain the lead and no further opportunity to defeat the contract, for the complete deal was as follows:

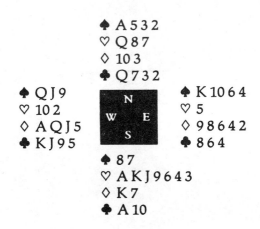

```
              ♠ A 5 3 2
              ♡ Q 8 7
              ◊ 10 3
              ♣ Q 7 3 2
♠ Q J 9                       ♠ K 10 6 4
♡ 10 2                        ♡ 5
◊ A Q J 5                     ◊ 9 8 6 4 2
♣ K J 9 5                     ♣ 8 6 4
              ♠ 8 7
              ♡ A K J 9 6 4 3
              ◊ K 7
              ♣ A 10
```

The declarer won the second spade, drew trumps in two rounds, and played the ace and another club to establish a second trick in the suit and a parking place for one of his losing diamonds.

In the other room East was awake and overtook his partner's queen of spades with the king in order to shoot back a diamond. West took two diamond tricks and switched back to spades, and the declarer was unable to avoid the loss of a further trick in clubs.

MAXIM.   Keep awake in defense, for there will often be no second chance.

---

7. DANGEROUS PASS

Overcalling on a four-card suit when vulnerable is a dangerous practice that can lead to four-figure penalties. But danger is a relative matter, and there are many hands on which it is much more dangerous to pass than to bid. Here is a typical example.

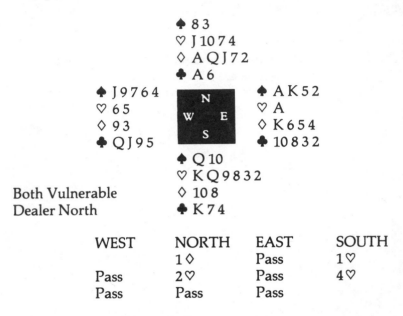

	♠ 83		
	♡ J 10 7 4		
	◊ A Q J 7 2		
	♣ A 6		

♠ J 9 7 6 4		♠ A K 5 2
♡ 6 5		♡ A
◊ 9 3		◊ K 6 5 4
♣ Q J 9 5		♣ 10 8 3 2

	♠ Q 10
	♡ K Q 9 8 3 2
Both Vulnerable	◊ 10 8
Dealer North	♣ K 7 4

WEST	NORTH	EAST	SOUTH
	1 ◊	Pass	1 ♡
Pass	2 ♡	Pass	4 ♡
Pass	Pass	Pass	

East decided against making a vulnerable overall of one spade on his four-card suit and his opponents bid to game without interference.

Having no good reason to choose a spade or a diamond, West made the natural lead of the queen of clubs. The declarer was quick to spot his extra chance. He won with the ace, played a second club to his king and ruffed the third club in dummy. A trump from the table then left East in a hopeless position. After cashing the top spades he had to choose between conceding a ruff and discard and leading a diamond away from his king. Either way, the declarer was bound to make ten tricks.

An overcall is often worth making for no other reason than to indicate a good lead. Here an initial spade lead would have enabled East to cash two spades and the ace of hearts. After exiting safely in clubs, East could then sit back and wait to score the setting trick with his king of diamonds.

East had a further chance to enter the auction by doubling two hearts for takeout on the second round. This would not have had quite the same lead-directional effect, but it might have led to a sound sacrifice.

Sacrifice? Four spades is in fact a pretty fair contract for East and West — a contract that will make if the opponents fail to find their club ruff.

MAXIM. Put in an overcall to indicate a good lead.

8. DANGEROUS BID

Aggressive players like to launch themselves into the bidding whenever they can and sometimes fall into the tactical error of making shaded overcalls on weak suits. The danger of this practice is highlighted by the happenings on the following hand from a team game.

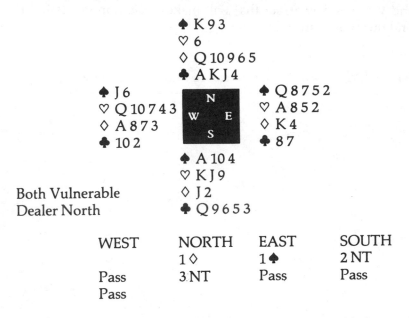

♠ K 9 3
♡ 6
◊ Q 10 9 6 5
♣ A K J 4

♠ J 6
♡ Q 10 7 4 3
◊ A 8 7 3
♣ 10 2

♠ Q 8 7 5 2
♡ A 8 5 2
◊ K 4
♣ 8 7

♠ A 10 4
♡ K J 9
◊ J 2
♣ Q 9 6 5 3

Both Vulnerable
Dealer North

WEST	NORTH	EAST	SOUTH
	1 ◊	1 ♠	2 NT
Pass	3 NT	Pass	Pass
Pass			

Light overcalls are all very well, but they are likely to do more harm than good if they have no lead-directional value. If East could not bear to pass on the first round he would have been better advised to make a Michaels cue bid. The overcall of one spade asked for a lead that East did not really want, thereby snatching defeat from the jaws of victory.

Respecting his partner's overcall, West rejected the natural heart lead in favor of the jack of spades. Dummy's king won the trick, and although East played the two the damage had been done. The declarer played a low diamond at trick two and the jack was captured by the ace. West found the heart switch, but South scored his king on the second round, entered dummy with a club, and finessed successfully in spades for his ninth trick.

22

The same contract was reached without interference in the other room, but on the normal heart lead the declarer had no chance of making more than eight tricks.

Note that only the spade lead is fatal. On a neutral diamond or club lead, the defenders have only to find the heart switch to defeat the game.

MAXIM. Avoid overcalling when you can't stand the lead.

---

9. TIMING THE RUFF

A good 5-3 trump fit inspires confidence, but declarer may all too easily lose control if he allows his trumps to be shortened at an early stage in the play. Look at what happened on this hand.

```
              ♠ Q 7 4
              ♡ 8 3
              ◇ K 7 6 2
              ♣ Q 10 8 5

                  N
              W       E
                  S

              ♠ A K J 8 3
              ♡ 5
              ◇ A 9 4 3
              ♣ K J 2
```

Both Vulnerable
Dealer South

SOUTH	WEST	NORTH	EAST
1♠	2♡	2♠	4♡
4♠	Pass	Pass	Pass

West led the queen of hearts to his partner's king and South ruffed the heart return. Game looked easy with five trumps, two diamonds and three clubs, but the snag became apparent when West discarded a club on the second round of trumps. If the remaining trumps were drawn, the defenders would be in a position to cash far too many hearts when in with the ace of clubs.

South tried to overcome the problem by switching to clubs after two rounds of trumps, but the defenders were not so obliging as to take the ace immediately. The king of clubs was allowed to win, but West took his ace of clubs on the second round and played a third club for his partner to ruff. South still had an unavoidable loser in diamonds and the contract went one down.

The complete deal:

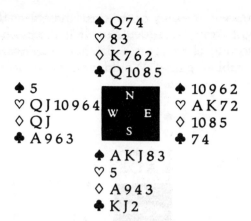

```
                    ♠ Q 7 4
                    ♡ 8 3
                    ◇ K 7 6 2
                    ♣ Q 10 8 5
  ♠ 5                                ♠ 10 9 6 2
  ♡ Q J 10 9 6 4         N           ♡ A K 7 2
  ◇ Q J            W         E       ◇ 10 8 5
  ♣ A 9 6 3             S             ♣ 7 4
                    ♠ A K J 8 3
                    ♡ 5
                    ◇ A 9 4 3
                    ♣ K J 2
```

Note the difference if South discards a diamond on the second heart instead of ruffing. This loser-on-loser play gives complete protection against the 4-1 trump break. If the defenders play a third heart the ruff can be taken in dummy, preserving South's trump holding intact. After drawing trumps, South can knock out the ace of clubs and claim the ten tricks that are rightfully his.

MAXIM. When you can afford it, discard a loser rather than allow your long trumps to be forced.

---

10. A CHANCE TO SHINE

An opportunity in the play of the cards may be as fleeting as a shaft of sunlight from a clouded sky. If it is missed there will often be no second chance, as a defender discovered on this hand from a rubber game. Would you have defeated three notrump?

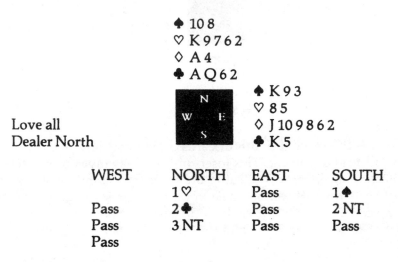

Love all
Dealer North

♠ 10 8
♡ K 9 7 6 2
◇ A 4
♣ A Q 6 2

♠ K 9 3
♡ 8 5
◇ J 10 9 8 6 2
♣ K 5

WEST	NORTH	EAST	SOUTH
	1♡	Pass	1♠
Pass	2♣	Pass	2 NT
Pass	3 NT	Pass	Pass
Pass			

West led the ten of clubs, the two was played from dummy and East won with the king. There was clearly no future in a club continuation since South was marked with three tricks in the suit. A switch was called for, and East made the natural return of the jack of diamonds.

Most players would have done the same, but in practice this switch enabled the declarer to run off ten straight tricks.

The complete deal:

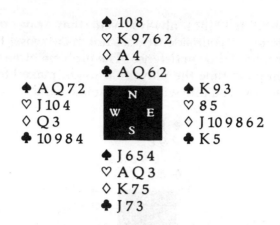

```
                 ♠ 10 8
                 ♡ K 9 7 6 2
                 ◊ A 4
                 ♣ A Q 6 2
♠ A Q 7 2          N          ♠ K 9 3
♡ J 10 4      W        E      ♡ 8 5
◊ Q 3            S          ◊ J 10 9 8 6 2
♣ 10 9 8 4                   ♣ K 5
                 ♠ J 6 5 4
                 ♡ A Q 3
                 ◊ K 7 5
                 ♣ J 7 3
```

In the light of the bidding there was not much point in that diamond switch. Even if East had been able to establish some diamond tricks there was virtually no possibility of regaining the lead to cash them. It is hard to imagine how the contract could be defeated unless the defenders could make some tricks in spades. East should therefore have switched to a spade in spite of the fact that declarer had bid the suit.

Any spade will not do. To keep alive the possibility of taking four fast tricks in the suit, East must lead the nine of spades. West wins the queen, returns the two to his partner's king, and scores two further spade tricks with the ace and the seven. Not an easy defense, to be sure, but a very satisfying one to achieve.

MAXIM. When switching, choose the suit that offers a real hope of beating the contract.

---

11. SMOOTHING THE WAY

Although it may not always seem that way, partner is supposed to be on your side. It does not make sense, therefore, to give him a hard time in defense. The problem often is how to recognize in good time the plays that might make life difficult for him. See how you fare with this example hand.

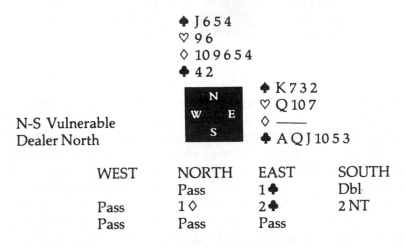

♠ J 6 5 4
♡ 9 6
♢ 10 9 6 5 4
♣ 4 2

♠ K 7 3 2
♡ Q 10 7
♢ —
♣ A Q J 10 5 3

N-S Vulnerable
Dealer North

WEST	NORTH	EAST	SOUTH
	Pass	1♣	Dbl
Pass	1♢	2♣	2 NT
Pass	Pass	Pass	

West leads the eight of clubs on which East plays the ten and South the six. How should East continue?

Dummy is almost featureless and it must be highly unlikely that declarer can make the contract. It seems absolutely normal to continue with the ace and another club. It there anything to be said against this defense?

In practice East did continue with the ace and another club — and the declarer made his contract. East can hardly be said to have committed a serious blunder, but he did oblige his partner to find a discard on the third round of clubs.

A glance at the full hand will show the severity of West's problem.

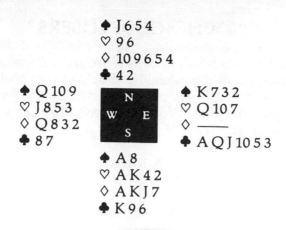

♠ J 6 5 4
♥ 9 6
♦ 10 9 6 5 4
♣ 4 2

♠ Q 10 9
♥ J 8 5 3
♦ Q 8 3 2
♣ 8 7

♠ K 7 3 2
♥ Q 10 7
♦ ———
♣ A Q J 10 5 3

♠ A 8
♥ A K 4 2
♦ A K J 7
♣ K 9 6

West could in fact spare a spade on the third round of clubs but it was hard for him to see this. Instead he made the natural discard of a diamond, after which there was no defense. South knocked out the queen of diamonds and was able to put together one spade, two hearts, four diamonds and a club.

West's fourth diamond was needed to prevent declarer from establishing the long diamond in dummy. If West throws a spade on the third club he can hold up the queen of diamonds until the fourth round. East, meanwhile, can discard two spades and two hearts on the diamonds, and the declarer is held to seven tricks.

There was no need for East to punish his partner in this way. It is a simple matter to return the queen or the jack of clubs at trick two, without cashing the ace. West then has no discard problem and the contract is easily defeated.

MAXIM.   Don't force partner to make unnecessary discards.

---

12. CHOICE OF LOSERS

There are certain hands on which declarer can choose to lose tricks in one suit or the other. He should always prefer to lose tricks in a suit that holds out the possibility of developing a winner at the same time. Would you have done any better than declarer on this hand?

♠ K 10 6 4
♡ A Q 7 2
♢ 7
♣ K 10 8 3

	N	
W		E
	S	

♠ Q J 9 7 5 2
♡ 6 5 3
♢ A K 6
♣ 9

Both Vulnerable
Dealer East

WEST	NORTH	EAST	SOUTH
		1 NT	2 ♠
Pass	4 ♠	Pass	Pass
Pass			

West led the four of clubs and South played low from dummy. East won with the queen and returned the ten of diamonds. South took his ace, ruffed the small diamond in dummy and returned a low spade. East went up with the ace and continued with a second spade, on which West discarded a diamond. South won in hand, cashed the king of diamonds, throwing a heart from dummy, and played a heart, hoping to duck the trick to East. He was out of luck, for the complete deal was as follows:

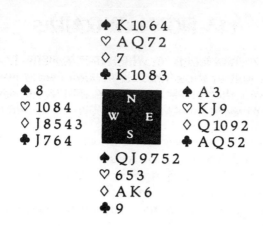

```
                  ♠ K 10 6 4
                  ♡ A Q 7 2
                  ◇ 7
                  ♣ K 10 8 3
   ♠ 8                         ♠ A 3
   ♡ 10 8 4        N           ♡ K J 9
   ◇ J 8 5 4 3   W   E         ◇ Q 10 9 2
   ♣ J 7 6 4       S           ♣ A Q 5 2
                  ♠ Q J 9 7 5 2
                  ♡ 6 5 3
                  ◇ A K 6
                  ♣ 9
```

South might have succeeded against a lazy defense, but West was on the ball and put in the ten of hearts on the first round. This made it impossible for South to avoid the loss of two hearts and the contract.

This is really a simple hand. South had nine tricks from the start and needed to find a tenth in either hearts or clubs. The chances in hearts were nebulous since East was marked with the king. In clubs, however, declarer should have been confident of establishing his tenth trick. East was bound to have the ace for his opening bid. All South had to do was to win the second trump in dummy, play the king of clubs, ruffing out the ace, returning to dummy with a trump and play the ten of clubs, discarding a heart from his hand. West would win with the jack and switch to a heart, but South could win with the ace and discard his remaining heart loser on the established eight of clubs.

MAXIM.   When losing tricks to the defenders, try at the same time to establish tricks for yourself.

---

13. SIGNALING AID

There are still some players who refuse to signal in defense on the grounds that it gives away too much information to the declarer. This may be true enough in particular cases, but on balance the winning policy is to help partner by signaling loud and clear.

Distributional echoes are useful in many situations. The idea is that when a defender is not trying to win a trick he should play high-low with an even number of cards in the suit and low-high with an odd number. A defender who can trust his partner to show distribution in this manner will not easily be deceived by the declarer.

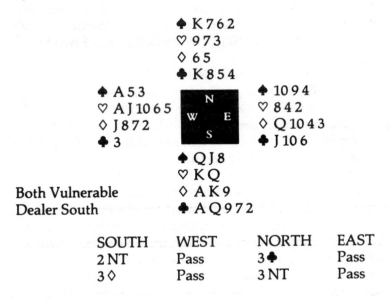

```
                    ♠ K 7 6 2
                    ♡ 9 7 3
                    ◇ 6 5
                    ♣ K 8 5 4
       ♠ A 5 3           N           ♠ 10 9 4
       ♡ A J 10 6 5   W     E        ♡ 8 4 2
       ◇ J 8 7 2         S           ◇ Q 10 4 3
       ♣ 3                            ♣ J 10 6
                    ♠ Q J 8
                    ♡ K Q
Both Vulnerable     ◇ A K 9
Dealer South        ♣ A Q 9 7 2
```

SOUTH	WEST	NORTH	EAST
2 NT	Pass	3 ♣	Pass
3 ◇	Pass	3 NT	Pass

Five clubs would have been a simpler contract, but South played in three notrump and West led the jack of hearts to the three and queen. Needing to steal a ninth trick in spades, the declarer first played a club to dummy's king and returned a club to his ace. When West discarded a diamond South paused for a moment (quite unethically) as though digesting the news of a bad club break. Then he played the jack of spades.

Without the help of distributional signals West might well have done the wrong thing by playing low. However, he knew that his partner's two of hearts at trick one indicated an odd number of cards in the suit. A singleton could be ruled out since South had denied four hearts in the bidding, so West was left with the certainty that East had started with three small hearts and South with the king and queen doubleton.

The correct defense was marked. West took his ace of spades on the first round and continued with the ace of hearts to defeat the contract.

MAXIM. Help partner by signaling your distribution.

---

14. APPLYING PRESSURE

There is a simple ploy that is worth remembering when you appear to be a trick short in a notrump contract. If there is a long, solid suit in the hand, play it out before surrendering the lead. You never know what may happen. It is not necessary to know anything about squeeze technique. Just play out the cards and hope for the best. The stratagem produced a game swing on this hand from a match.

```
              ♠ A K J 10 3
              ♡ Q 4
              ◇ K 9 8 5 2
              ♣ 7
                  N
               W     E
                  S
              ♠ Q 5
              ♡ K J 9 6 2
Both Vulnerable   ◇ A 10
Dealer West       ♣ Q 10 9 4
```

WEST	NORTH	EAST	SOUTH
Pass	1♠	Pass	2♡
Pass	2♣	Pass	2 NT
Pass	3◇	Pass	3 NT
Pass	Pass	Pass	

The contract was the same in both rooms and the defenders attacked in clubs. East took the first two tricks with the king and ace, and South won the third round with the queen as dummy discarded two diamonds. There were eight top tricks and the declarers could hope to establish extra tricks in hearts.

In one room, the declarer saw nothing better than to do than to play a small heart at trick four, hoping that East would have the ace or that the clubs would break 4-4. This did not work out since the complete deal was as follows:

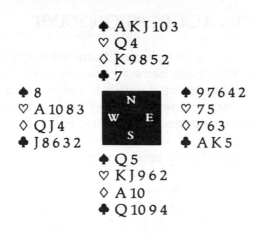

```
                    ♠ A K J 10 3
                    ♡ Q 4
                    ◊ K 9 8 5 2
                    ♣ 7
    ♠ 8                             ♠ 9 7 6 4 2
    ♡ A 10 8 3         N           ♡ 7 5
    ◊ Q J 4        W       E       ◊ 7 6 3
    ♣ J 8 6 3 2        S           ♣ A K 5
                    ♠ Q 5
                    ♡ K J 9 6 2
                    ◊ A 10
                    ♣ Q 10 9 4
```

West gratefully took the ace of hearts and cashed two more clubs to put the contract one down.

In the other room the declarer was alive to the danger of losing four clubs and a heart. After winning the queen of clubs he continued with five rounds of spades, discarding two hearts and the ten of clubs from his hand. West was able to part with three hearts without pain, but the play of the fifth spade had him in trouble. It was clear that a club discard would allow the declarer to knock out the ace of hearts with impunity. West therefore chose to throw a diamond in the hope that his partner had the ten.

That was all the help South needed. He played a diamond to his ace and returned the suit. The fall of the queen and jack gave him nine tricks and a swing of 12 IMP's.

MAXIM. When you appear to be a trick short, try the effect of playing out the long suit.

---

15. AGGRESSION PAYS

When you hold a semi-balanced hand with about 20 high-card points, the choice lies between opening quietly with a bid of one in a suit or aggressively with a bid of two notrump. One reason for favoring the opening bid of two notrump is that it sometimes has an unexpected pre-emptive effect.

Here is an example from a team game.

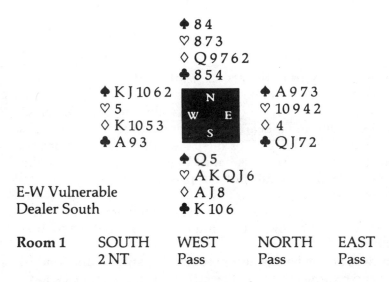

```
                    ♠ 8 4
                    ♡ 8 7 3
                    ◊ Q 9 7 6 2
                    ♣ 8 5 4
    ♠ K J 10 6 2                    ♠ A 9 7 3
    ♡ 5              N              ♡ 10 9 4 2
    ◊ K 10 5 3    W     E          ◊ 4
    ♣ A 9 3          S              ♣ Q J 7 2
                    ♠ Q 5
                    ♡ A K Q J 6
E-W Vulnerable      ◊ A J 8
Dealer South        ♣ K 10 6
```

Room 1	SOUTH	WEST	NORTH	EAST
	2 NT	Pass	Pass	Pass

It was hardly possible for anyone to bid over the opening bid of two notrump. West led a spade and the contract went quietly down for a score of 100 to East and West.

Room 2	SOUTH	WEST	NORTH	EAST
	1 ♡	1 ♠	Pass	3 ♠
	Pass	4 ♠	Pass	Pass
	Pass			

In the other room the opening bid of one heart gave West the chance to come in at a low level, and a distributional game contract was quickly reached.

Taking the right view in trumps, West had no difficulty in making ten tricks, losing just one heart, one diamond and one

36

club. That was worth 620 and a gain of 11 IMP's.

MAXIM.   **Be aggressive in choosing your opening bid.**

---

16. IT'S A STEAL

Defenders need to keep wide awake against a declarer who knows all the dodges. The following hand shows the declarer stealing a contract that is not really in the cards, and it is by no means an isolated case.

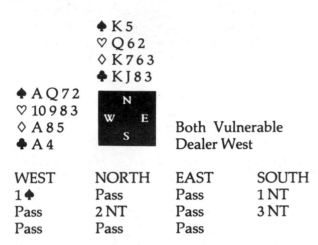

♠ K 5
♡ Q 6 2
◇ K 7 6 3
♣ K J 8 3

♠ A Q 7 2
♡ 10 9 8 3
◇ A 8 5
♣ A 4

Both Vulnerable
Dealer West

WEST	NORTH	EAST	SOUTH
1♣	Pass	Pass	1 NT
Pass	2 NT	Pass	3 NT
Pass	Pass	Pass	

On the lead of the ten of hearts East played the five and South the ace. The jack of diamonds was tabled at trick two and West automatically played low, half expecting the jack to run to his partner's queen. The jack of diamonds held the trick, however, and the declarer promptly switched to clubs. West took his ace and played the ace and another spade, but it was too late. The declarer was able to cash four club tricks, three hearts and one spade, and the stolen diamond trick made his tally up to nine.

The complete deal:

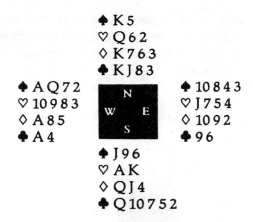

```
                    ♠ K 5
                    ♡ Q 6 2
                    ◇ K 7 6 3
                    ♣ K J 8 3
   ♠ A Q 7 2            N            ♠ 1 0 8 4 3
   ♡ 1 0 9 8 3     W        E        ♡ J 7 5 4
   ◇ A 8 5                            ◇ 1 0 9 2
   ♣ A 4                 S            ♣ 9 6
                    ♠ J 9 6
                    ♡ A K
                    ◇ Q J 4
                    ♣ Q 1 0 7 5 2
```

The declarer played well, certainly. Realizing that there would be five potential losers if he knocked out the ace of clubs immediately, he set out to steal a diamond trick before the defenders knew what was going on.

But West should not have been taken in. East could hardly have the queen of diamonds on the bidding, and West should have recognized that he needed to play the ace of diamonds on the jack and switch to spades. The defenders thus develop five tricks before the declarer can make nine.

MAXIM.   Don't let them steal you blind.

---

17. BACKING THE FAVORITE

At the race-track punters seldom accept anything less than the best odds available, but the same does not seem to apply at the bridge table. On this hand from a match one declarer put his money on the wrong horse.

♠ 9 7 6 3 2
♡ A Q J
◇ 10 4
♣ 9 5 3

```
      N
   W     E
      S
```

♠ A 10
♡ K 10 6 2
◇ A Q 5 2
♣ A K 6

N-S Vulnerable
Dealer South

SOUTH	WEST	NORTH	EAST
2 NT	Pass	3♠	Pass
3 NT	Pass	Pass	Pass

The bidding was the same in both rooms, as was the opening lead of the nine of hearts. One declarer won in dummy and went after the spades, playing the ace and another. East won with the queen and switched to the queen of clubs. South took his ace, crossed to dummy in hearts and played another spade. East discarded a diamond on this trick, and when West won he returned a heart to take out dummy's last entry. South then had to fall back on a finesse of the queen of diamonds, and when this failed so did the contract.

The complete deal:

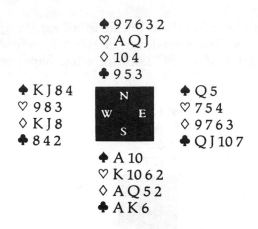

```
                  ♠ 9 7 6 3 2
                  ♡ A Q J
                  ◇ 10 4
                  ♣ 9 5 3
  ♠ K J 8 4          N           ♠ Q 5
  ♡ 9 8 3                        ♡ 7 5 4
  ◇ K J 8        W     E         ◇ 9 7 6 3
  ♣ 8 4 2           S            ♣ Q J 10 7
                  ♠ A 10
                  ♡ K 10 6 2
                  ◇ A Q 5 2
                  ♣ A K 6
```

South would have succeeded if the spades had split 3-3 or if the diamond finesse had been right, giving him an overall chance of 68%. But better odds were on offer as was demonstrated in the other room.

The declarer in the other room pinned his faith on the diamond suit. He won the heart lead in hand, overtaking dummy's jack with his king, and played a low diamond toward the ten. West won with the jack and switched to a club, but South took his ace, unblocked the hearts and ran the ten of diamonds. West was able to win, but declarer had established a second diamond trick giving him nine tricks altogether.

South's plan depended on finding either the jack of diamonds in the West hand or the king of diamonds with East — a total chance of 74%. Clearly he backed the favorite.

MAXIM. **Learn your percentages and accept nothing less than the best odds available.**

18. WITHOUT FINESSE

Players learn how to take a finesse at an early stage in their bridge education. The knowledge of when to refuse a finesse comes much later, if at all. Look at what happened on this hand.

♠ K Q 8 4
♡ A Q 7 4
◊ 5 3
♣ K 7 5

```
       N
   W       E
       S
```

♠ J 10 3
♡ J 5
◊ K J 10 6
♣ A Q J 4

Love all
Dealer South

SOUTH	WEST	NORTH	EAST
1 NT*	Pass	2♣	Pass
2◊	Pass	3 NT	Pass
Pass	Pass		

* 12-14 HCP

The normal contract of three notrump was quickly reached and the three of hearts was led. How should South play?

Hoping to make three tricks in the suit and seeing no danger, South played low from dummy. East won with the king and promptly switched to the eight of diamonds. Still, confident, South put in the ten, but he began to feel a little uneasy when West won with the queen and returned the four of diamonds to the seven and jack.

At this point South had eight tricks and needed a spade trick for his contract. He hoped to sneak past the ace, but East produced the ace of spades and returned a diamond to give his partner two further tricks in the suit.

42

The full hand:

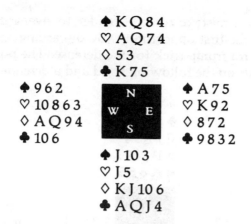

```
                 ♠ K Q 8 4
                 ♡ A Q 7 4
                 ◊ 5 3
                 ♣ K 7 5
    ♠ 9 6 2          N          ♠ A 7 5
    ♡ 10 8 6 3    W     E       ♡ K 9 2
    ◊ A Q 9 4        S          ◊ 8 7 2
    ♣ 10 6                      ♣ 9 8 3 2
                 ♠ J 10 3
                 ♡ J 5
                 ◊ K J 10 6
                 ♣ A Q J 4
```

South's troubles were all of his own making, of course. Finessing in hearts at trick one was an expensive blunder of the type often made by players who do not bother to count their tricks. A finesse should never be taken when it puts a lay-down contract at risk. The correct play is to put up the ace of hearts at trick one and knock out the ace of spades. This establishes eight tricks, and a ninth is bound to be made in one of the red suits.

MAXIM.   **Never take an unnecessary finesse.**

---

19. TROUBLESOME TRUMPS

It is usually a mistake for a defender to over-ruff with an honor card at the first opportunity. By discarding he may well promote an extra trump trick for the defense. The position was not too obvious on the following hand and a defender fell from grace.

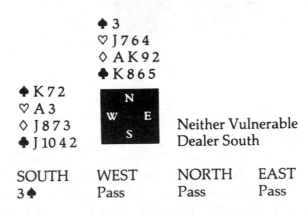

```
                    ♠ 3
                    ♡ J 7 6 4
                    ◊ A K 9 2
                    ♣ K 8 6 5
        ♠ K 7 2
        ♡ A 3
        ◊ J 8 7 3              Neither Vulnerable
        ♣ J 10 4 2            Dealer South
```

SOUTH	WEST	NORTH	EAST
3♠	Pass	Pass	Pass

West led the ace of hearts and East encouraged with the ten. The nine of hearts won the second trick, and East continued with the queen of hearts which was ruffed by South with the ten of spades.

Seeing little chance of promoting a second trump, West over-ruffed with the king and switched to the jack of clubs. East won with the ace and continued with the king of hearts, but South was able to ruff high, draw the remaining trumps and claim nine tricks.

Even a seven can be promoted now and then. If West had refused to over-ruff on the third round of hearts the contract would have been defeated, for the complete deal was as follows:

44

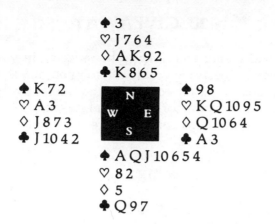

```
              ♠ 3
              ♡ J 7 6 4
              ◊ A K 9 2
              ♣ K 8 6 5
  ♠ K 7 2                    ♠ 9 8
  ♡ A 3          N           ♡ K Q 10 9 5
  ◊ J 8 7 3    W   E         ◊ Q 10 6 4
  ♣ J 10 4 2     S           ♣ A 3
              ♠ A Q J 10 6 5 4
              ♡ 8 2
              ◊ 5
              ♣ Q 9 7
```

If West had discarded on the third heart, South would have continued with the ace and queen of spades. West takes his king, puts his partner in with the ace of clubs, and a further heart lead promotes a trick for the seven of spades.

West claimed that failing to over-ruff might have cost the contract, allowing declarer to discard a club loser on dummy's diamonds. Do you see the flaw in his reasoning?

If South had held the hand that West feared — a 7-2-2-2 shape with more solid spades and the queen of diamonds — he would not have given West the opportunity to defeat him. He would have ruffed the third heart with the ace of spades and played three or four rounds of diamonds for club discards.

MAXIM. Refuse to over-ruff with a trump honor in the hope of promoting an extra trump trick.

---

20. GIVEAWAY

Do you allow your emotions to be reflected in your face or your manner at the bridge table? If so, you are at a big disadvantage. You might try to correct the failing by taking part in a weekly poker session for substantial stakes.

A defender's failure to control his feelings proved expensive on the following hand.

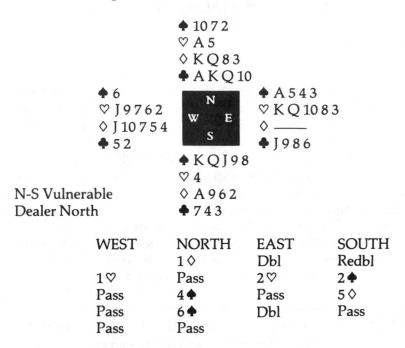

```
                  ♠ 10 7 2
                  ♡ A 5
                  ◊ K Q 8 3
                  ♣ A K Q 10
   ♠ 6                          ♠ A 5 4 3
   ♡ J 9 7 6 2                  ♡ K Q 10 8 3
   ◊ J 10 7 5 4                 ◊ ——
   ♣ 5 2                        ♣ J 9 8 6
                  ♠ K Q J 9 8
                  ♡ 4
   N-S Vulnerable ◊ A 9 6 2
   Dealer North   ♣ 7 4 3
```

WEST	NORTH	EAST	SOUTH
	1◊	Dbl	Redbl
1♡	Pass	2♡	2♠
Pass	4♠	Pass	5◊
Pass	6♣	Dbl	Pass
Pass	Pass		

Everyone had something to say in the auction and South eventually played in six spades. East doubled for a diamond lead, but West failed to get the message and led the six of hearts. This might not have been disastrous but for the fact that East slapped his cards down on the table in a gesture of annoyance.

Left in no doubt that East was void in diamonds, the declarer was able to plan the play on double-dummy lines. Winning the first trick with the ace of hearts, he knocked out the trump ace, ruffed the heart continuation and drew the remaining trumps.

The 4-1 trump break was a bit of an embarrassment for South had to make a discard from dummy on the fourth trump.

Instead of a normal diamond South threw the ten of clubs, relying solely on the diamond suit for his twelfth trick. The shortage of entries to hand made it impossible to test the diamonds by cashing the ace first, but South was sufficiently confident of the position to play a low diamond from hand and finesse dummy's eight on the first round. Thus the doubled slam was landed.

It is possible that South would have found the winning line in any case, but East's display of temper certainly made things easy for him.

MAXIM.	Keep your emotions under control at all times.

21. RUFF TREATMENT

The best of contracts may be upset by an enemy ruff, but sometimes it is possible for the declarer to take counter-measures. Here is an example from a team game.

♠ Q 10 7 2
♡ 9 7
♢ J 4
♣ A K Q 9 2

```
      N
   W     E
      S
```

♠ K J 9 6 5
♡ A K 2
♢ 7 5
♣ J 4 3

Neither Vulnerable
Dealer North

WEST	NORTH	EAST	SOUTH
	1♣	1♢	1♠
Pass	2♠	Pass	4♠
Pass	Pass	Pass	

West led the king of diamonds which East overtook with the ace in order to return the eight of clubs. How should South plan the play?

At one table the declarer saw nothing better than to try and slip past the ace of trumps. He won the club switch in dummy and played the two of spades, but East was not tempted to play low. He won the ace of spades, put his partner in with the queen of diamonds and received a club ruff to put the contract one down.

The complete deal:

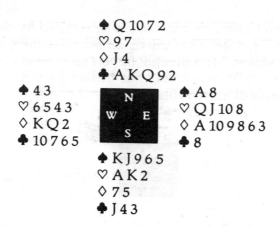

```
              ♠ Q 10 7 2
              ♡ 9 7
              ◇ J 4
              ♣ A K Q 9 2
♠ 4 3              N              ♠ A 8
♡ 6 5 4 3      W       E          ♡ Q J 10 8
◇ K Q 2            S              ◇ A 10 9 8 6 3
♣ 10 7 6 5                        ♣ 8
              ♠ K J 9 6 5
              ♡ A K 2
              ◇ 7 5
              ♣ J 4 3
```

In the other room the declarer diagnosed the danger correctly and came up with a neat counter. Before touching trumps he played out the ace, king and two of hearts, discarding the jack of diamonds from the table. East had to win the trick, and since he was unable to pass the lead to his partner the contract was safe.

South was lucky in that West was unable to win the third round of hearts, but he earned his luck by seizing his chance. Anything is better than sitting back and meekly awaiting the chopper.

This type of play, where the declarer escapes from a threatened ruff by cutting the enemy communications, is aptly named the scissors coup.

MAXIM.   Look out for a chance to use the scissors coup when an enemy ruff is threatened.

---

22. LEADING QUESTION

The fate of countless contracts is determined by the opening lead, which can be a hazardous affair when there is no help from the bidding. West thought he was unlucky in his choice of lead on the following hand, but in fact he was guilty of a common error of judgement.

♠ 974
♡ A J 8 2
◊ Q 10 7 3
♣ 8 2

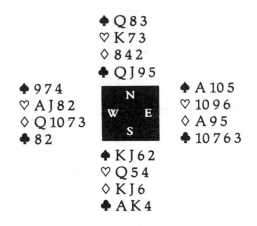

Neither Vulnerable
Dealer South

SOUTH	WEST	NORTH	EAST
1 NT	Pass	2 NT	Pass
3 NT	Pass	Pass	Pass

Most players know better than to underlead an ace in a suit contract, but it is a different matter against notrump. West had been schooled to lead from his longest and strongest suit, and he tabled the two of hearts without much pause for thought. This lead was not exactly a roaring success, as a glance at the full hand will show.

```
                    ♠ Q 8 3
                    ♡ K 7 3
                    ◊ 8 4 2
                    ♣ Q J 9 5
   ♠ 9 7 4                          ♠ A 10 5
   ♡ A J 8 2           N            ♡ 10 9 6
   ◊ Q 10 7 3      W       E        ◊ A 9 5
   ♣ 8 2               S            ♣ 10 7 6 3
                    ♠ K J 6 2
                    ♡ Q 5 4
                    ◊ K J 6
                    ♣ A K 4
```

The heart lead went to the nine and queen, and after

knocking out the ace of spades the declarer romped home with three spades tricks, two hearts and four clubs.

The lead from four cards headed by an ace is seldom productive and often costs a trick. When the opening leader has a choice between two suits of equal length, one headed by an ace and the other by a lower honor, it is almost always right to lead from the lower honor. The plan should be to establish the weaker suit while retaining the ace as an entry.

Note the difference if West starts with a diamond to his partner's ace. A normal diamond continuation, or even a heart shift, defeats the contract with ease.

In another setting the lead from the queen of diamonds might cost a trick, it is true, but in that event the defenders might get a second bite at the cherry. East will have an entry somewhere and if the diamond attack proves abortive the defense may still score four heart tricks on the switch.

MAXIM. Even at notrump, avoid leading from four cards headed by an ace.

---

23. RUFF NOW, PAY LATER

When the declarer has a two-suited hand, a forcing defense is called for and the defenders must guard against weakening their trump holding at an early stage. The best of players can have a blind spot when given the chance to over-ruff dummy. The following hand comes from a women's match in the European Championships many years ago.

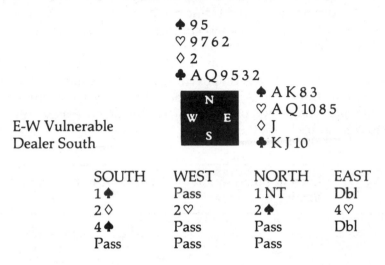

```
              ♠ 9 5
              ♡ 9 7 6 2
              ◇ 2
              ♣ A Q 9 5 3 2
                          ♠ A K 8 3
                 N          ♡ A Q 10 8 5
E-W Vulnerable  W   E       ◇ J
Dealer South     S          ♣ K J 10
```

SOUTH	WEST	NORTH	EAST
1♠	Pass	1 NT	Dbl
2◇	2♡	2♠	4♡
4♠	Pass	Pass	Dbl
Pass	Pass	Pass	

In both rooms South was doubled in four spades after East and West had bid to four hearts. South ruffed the initial heart lead and played the ace of diamonds followed by the three, ruffing in dummy with the nine of spades.

Both East players fell from grace by over-ruffing with the king of spades. They subsequently found that the contract could no longer be defeated, and the board was tied at 590 to North-South.

The complete deal:

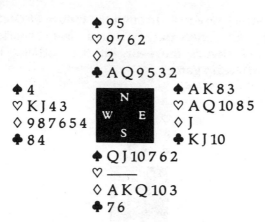

```
                    ♠ 9 5
                    ♡ 9 7 6 2
                    ◊ 2
                    ♣ A Q 9 5 3 2
   ♠ 4                              ♠ A K 8 3
   ♡ K J 4 3          N             ♡ A Q 10 8 5
   ◊ 9 8 7 6 5 4    W   E           ◊ J
   ♣ 8 4              S             ♣ K J 10
                    ♠ Q J 10 7 6 2
                    ♡ ——
                    ◊ A K Q 10 3
                    ♣ 7 6
```

This was really quite a surprising lapse on the part of the experts. East should, of course, discard a club instead of over-ruffing on the second round of diamonds. This play makes a difference of no fewer than three tricks to the defense.

When a trump is played at trick four East can win and punch declarer with a heart. In the end South makes no more than four trumps in his hand, one diamond, a diamond ruff and one club.

MAXIM.   Don't rush to over-ruff when you have length in trumps.

---

24. A MATTER OF URGENCY

Many contracts are lost through the failure of declarer to get his priorities right. There may be a great deal of work to do, but some jobs are always more urgent than others. Here is an example from a team game.

```
              ♠ J 5 3
              ♡ A Q J 6
              ◊ J 10 5
              ♣ Q 4 2
              ┌─────────┐
              │    N    │
              │  W   E  │
              │    S    │
              └─────────┘
              ♠ K 8 4
              ♡ 10 9 8 5 2
              ◊ K Q
              ♣ A K 5
```

Neither Vulnerable
Dealer South

SOUTH	WEST	NORTH	EAST
1 NT	Pass	2♣	Pass
2♡	Pass	4♡	Pass
Pass	Pass		

West led the jack of clubs and South won in hand with the king in order to tackle the trumps. He ran the ten of hearts to the king, and East, after a few moments' thought, placed the queen of spades on the table. This was a thoroughly alarming card, causing South to think, too late, about the need to dispose of one of his spade losers. At this stage South could only hope that the cards would be well placed for him. He covered the queen of spades with the king, which won the trick, then drew the remaining trumps, and played on diamonds. West had the diamond ace, however, and his spade return gave his partner two tricks in the suit.

The complete deal:

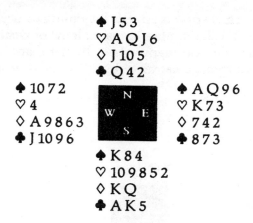

```
              ♠ J 5 3
              ♡ A Q J 6
              ◊ J 10 5
              ♣ Q 4 2
  ♠ 10 7 2            ♠ A Q 9 6
  ♡ 4         N       ♡ K 7 3
  ◊ A 9 8 6 3  W   E  ◊ 7 4 2
  ♣ J 10 9 6    S     ♣ 8 7 3
              ♠ K 8 4
              ♡ 10 9 8 5 2
              ◊ K Q
              ♣ A K 5
```

Good defense, but better timing by South would have denied East the chance to shine. South should recognize from the outset that there is no need for haste in the trump suit. The first task must be to knock out the ace of diamonds in order to establish a discard for one of the losing spades. By playing on diamonds South makes sure of the contract whenever West has the king of hearts or East has the ace of spades.

In the other room North declined to use Stayman on his flat hand, raising instead to three notrump. A spade lead defeats this contract (as it does four hearts) and even a club lead leaves the defense with a chance. West led a diamond, however, and the declarer could not be prevented from making nine tricks for a swing of 10 IMP's.

MAXIM.   Assign priorities and tackle the most urgent job first.

---

25. SELF-INFLICTED WOUNDS

Where bidding is concerned, the beginning of wisdom is the recognition of the right time to pass. It is especially vital to avoid making a bid too many when the hand appears to be a misfit. The point is illustrated by this hand from a pairs tournament.

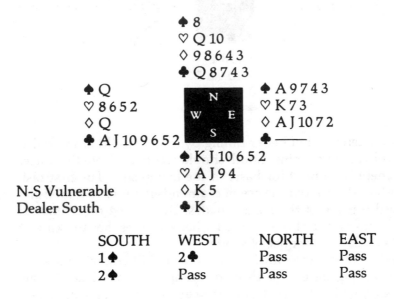

```
                        ♠ 8
                        ♡ Q 10
                        ◇ 9 8 6 4 3
                        ♣ Q 8 7 4 3
        ♠ Q                             ♠ A 9 7 4 3
        ♡ 8 6 5 2          N            ♡ K 7 3
        ◇ Q            W       E         ◇ A J 10 7 2
        ♣ A J 10 9 6 5 2    S            ♣ —
                        ♠ K J 10 6 5 2
                        ♡ A J 9 4
N-S Vulnerable          ◇ K 5
Dealer South            ♣ K
```

SOUTH	WEST	NORTH	EAST
1♠	2♣	Pass	Pass
2♠	Pass	Pass	Pass

The only table at which East-West registered a plus score was the one where the above auction took place. The other pairs invariably landed in trouble when East failed to appreciate that his hand, for all its twelve high-card points and fine distribution, was not worth a bid. Shortage in partner's suit and length in an opponent's suit are obvious danger signs, and East should realize that the hand is likely to be a death trap for the declaring side.

Against the contract of two spades West led the singleton diamond to his partner's ace. He ruffed the return of the two of diamonds with the spade queen, cashed the ace of clubs and continued with the jack of clubs. This was covered by the queen, ruffed by East with the seven of spades and over-ruffed by South with the ten.

The king of spades was allowed to win the next trick, and South had nothing better to do that continue with the six of spades. East won with the nine, cashed the ace of spades and got off lead with his remaining spade, eventually scoring his king of hearts as the setting trick.

MAXIM. Stop bidding as soon as there is evidence of a misfit.

26. WRAPPING IT UP

The road to success in defense lies in trying to reconstruct the concealed hands and workingout exactly what partner needs to have if the contract is to be defeated. The process often calls for the exercise of imagination.

```
              ♠ 9 6 5
              ♡ A 10 7
              ◊ A Q J 6 3
              ♣ K 4
                              ♠ Q 10 8 3
                    N         ♡ K 6 4
                  W   E       ◊ K 5
                    S         ♣ J 8 6 2
```

Neither Vulnerable
Dealer South

SOUTH	WEST	NORTH	EAST
Pass	Pass	1◊	Pass
2 NT	Pass	3 NT	Pass
Pass	Pass		

West led the three of hearts, the seven was played from dummy and East won with the king. How should he continue?

Instead of blindly returning his partner's suit, East took a moment to consider the position. On the bidding it seemed likely that South would have one of the heart honors, in which case a heart continuation could do nothing to advance the cause of the defense. In addition to the two red kings, the defenders need three tricks in one of the black suits to defeat the game.

Spades seemed to offer a better chance than clubs because South was marked with no more than three cards in the suit. East resolved to play for his partner to have one of the top spades, and in order to force an honor card from South he switched at trick two to the ten of spades.

This worked out well when the complete deal turned out to be:

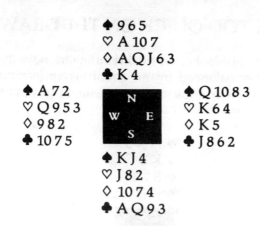

```
              ♠ 9 6 5
              ♡ A 10 7
              ◊ A Q J 6 3
              ♣ K 4
♠ A 7 2                      ♠ Q 10 8 3
♡ Q 9 5 3        N          ♡ K 6 4
◊ 9 8 2       W     E       ◊ K 5
♣ 10 7 5         S          ♣ J 8 6 2
              ♠ K J 4
              ♡ J 8 2
              ◊ 10 7 4
              ♣ A Q 9 3
```

South covered the ten of spades with the jack, but West won and continued the attack, establishing three spade tricks for the defense before declarer could get the diamonds going.

On the lie of the cards the play of the queen of spades at trick two does just as well, but the ten would be essential if South had the ace of spades and West the king.

MAXIM. When playing through declarer up to weakness in dummy, the card immediately above dummy's highest is the one to lead.

---

27. TOO QUICK ON THE DRAW

The number of players on the breadline because they did not draw trumps is balanced by an equal group in similar straits because they drew trumps too soon. Look at what happened on this hand.

```
                    ♠ A K 5
                    ♡ K 6
                    ◊ 8 7 3
                    ♣ K J 7 6 2
                         N
                    W         E
                         S
                    ♠ 9 7 4
                    ♡ 5
N-S Vulnerable      ◊ A K Q 6 4 2
Dealer West         ♣ 8 4 3
```

WEST	NORTH	EAST	SOUTH
1♡	Dbl	3♡	5◊
Pass	Pass	Pass	

West led the jack of spades and South saw with regret that three notrump by North would have been easier. Still, the cards were likely to be lying well and there was no reason why five diamonds should not come home.

Winning the spade lead, South tackled the diamonds. West discarded a heart on the second round, and South drew the third trump before leading a heart towards dummy's king. West took the ace and returned a spade to dummy. After discarding his third spade on the king of hearts, South ruffed a spade and then played a club to dummy's jack. This held the trick, but declarer was stuck in dummy with no way back to his hand for another club lead. When he tried a low club from the table, West won with the queen and cashed the ace to put the contract one down.

The complete hand:

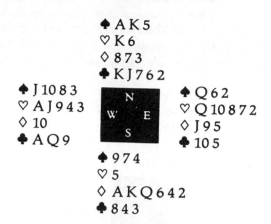

♠ A K 5
♥ K 6
♦ 8 7 3
♣ K J 7 6 2

♠ J 10 8 3
♥ A J 9 4 3
♦ 10
♣ A Q 9

♠ Q 6 2
♥ Q 10 8 7 2
♦ J 9 5
♣ 10 5

♠ 9 7 4
♥ 5
♦ A K Q 6 4 2
♣ 8 4 3

South was defeated because he squandered his trump entries. It is usually a good idea to draw the enemy trumps, but it may be necessary to postpone the operation when entries are short in the long trump hand. In this case South could see that he needed three entries in hand for one heart lead and two club leads. These entries could come only from the trump suit.

When West showed out on the second round of trumps, South should have abandoned the trump suit for the moment in favor of a heart lead. He could win the spade return, discard the spade loser on the heart king, and then draw the third round of trumps. A club to dummy's jack would then have left him in complete control, able to return to hand with a spade ruff for another club lead.

MAXIM. Delay drawing trumps when you need the trumps as entries.

---

28. EYE OFF BALL

It is the simplest thing in the world for a declarer to put a cold contract on the floor when his mind is cluttered with irrelevances. The declarer lost sight of his proper task on the following hand.

```
              ♠ K Q 9 4
              ♡ 9 3
              ◊ Q
              ♣ 10 9 7 6 5 3
                   N
               W       E
                   S
              ♠ A J 10 8 2
              ♡ A 8 5
E-W Vulnerable     ◊ K 7 6 2
Dealer South   ♣ 8
```

SOUTH	WEST	NORTH	EAST
1♠	Dbl	4♠	Pass
Pass	Pass		

West led a trump and at trick two South played a low diamond from hand, intent on setting up a diamond trick to take care of the losing heart in dummy. West took the ace of diamonds and returned another trump, the suit breaking 2-2. Declarer duly discarded a heart from dummy on the king of diamonds, but he could muster no more than nine tricks — seven trumps, one heart and one diamond. There was no possibility of a tenth trick, and the contract had to go one down.

The complete hand:

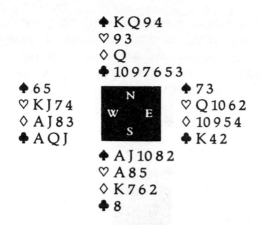

```
                ♠ K Q 9 4
                ♡ 9 3
                ◊ Q
                ♣ 10 9 7 6 5 3
  ♠ 6 5            N          ♠ 7 3
  ♡ K J 7 4                   ♡ Q 10 6 2
  ◊ A J 8 3     W     E       ◊ 10 9 5 4
  ♣ A Q J          S          ♣ K 4 2
                ♠ A J 10 8 2
                ♡ A 8 5
                ◊ K 7 6 2
                ♣ 8
```

All one can say is that South was the victim of an illusion on this hand. There could be no possible advantage in setting up the king of diamonds for a heart discard. South does not even need a diamond trick to make his game. All he needs is to find the clubs 3-3, but it is essential to start the clubs before a second round of trumps has been played.

The right move is to concede the club loser at trick two. West will win and return a trump, but South can win in dummy, ruff a club, and play a diamond to West's ace. Whatever West returns, South can discard a heart on the king of diamonds, ruff a diamond or a heart, and ruff another club to make dummy high. Correct play thus brings in eleven tricks, although South might be held to ten tricks if West switches to hearts at trick three.

MAXIM.   Ignore red herrings when planning the play.

---

29. TIMING THE DEFENSE

The bridge player learns at his mother's knee that the best lead against a notrump contract is the fourth-highest card of his longest and strongest suit. All such rules have their exceptions, however, and it is important to be able to recognize the right occasion for leading something else.

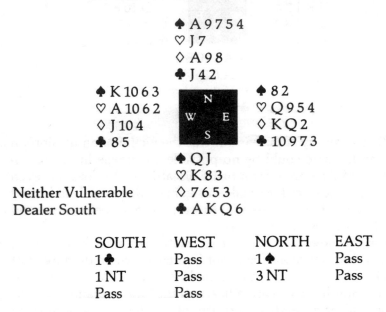

```
                        ♠ A 9 7 5 4
                        ♡ J 7
                        ◊ A 9 8
                        ♣ J 4 2
      ♠ K 10 6 3             N           ♠ 8 2
      ♡ A 10 6 2                          ♡ Q 9 5 4
      ◊ J 10 4        W         E        ◊ K Q 2
      ♣ 8 5                               ♣ 10 9 7 3
                            S
                        ♠ Q J
                        ♡ K 8 3
Neither Vulnerable      ◊ 7 6 5 3
Dealer South            ♣ A K Q 6
```

SOUTH	WEST	NORTH	EAST
1 ♣	Pass	1 ♠	Pass
1 NT	Pass	3 NT	Pass
Pass	Pass		

West is not likely to lead a spade once the suit has been bid on his left. Most players would automatically table the two of hearts, but this gives declarer an easy ride. With all the time he needs to establish the spade suit, South will make his contract with the loss of three hearts and one spade.

Experienced defenders try to avoid making an opening lead from four cards headed by an ace, for they know that all too often this gives up a vital tempo. Both in theory and in practice the jack of diamonds is a better choice on this hand.

The diamond lead launches an immediate attack on one of dummy's entries, but it does not automatically defeat the contract. If declarer ducks at trick one, as he should, East may be tempted to overtake his partner's jack and continue the suit, which is the wrong defense. Seeing the eight and nine of diamonds in dummy, East should realize that his partner has led from a short suit and should play the two of diamonds. This card will serve as a warning to West, helping him to realize that the time has come to switch to hearts.

If diamonds are continued at trick two South can make his contract. He takes the ace of diamonds and plays a third round. Now it is too late for a heart shift since this gives South his ninth trick. Suppose East shifts instead to a club. South wins in hand, plays the queen of spades to the king and ace and returns a spade to his jack, noting the fall of the eight. After throwing a heart from dummy on the thirteenth diamond, he cashes a high club and plays the six of clubs to dummy's jack. The nine of spades then puts West on lead, and South makes nine tricks whether a spade or a heart is returned.

MAXIM.   Try a short suit lead rather than concede a trick that declarer might not be able to get on his own.

---

30. LOCKOUT PLAY

There are times when the only way to shut out a long suit is to keep playing the suit until declarer loses touch with dummy. Here is an example:

```
                    ♠ 6 4
                    ♡ K 8 3
                    ◊ K Q J 10 5
                    ♣ J 10 3
   ♠ A Q 3                          
   ♡ Q J 10 6        N              
   ◊ 8 7 2        W     E           Both Vulnerable
   ♣ Q 7 5           S               Dealer South
```

SOUTH	WEST	NORTH	EAST
1 ♠	Pass	2 ◊	Pass
4 ♠	Pass	Pass	Pass

West led the queen of hearts on which dummy played the three, East the two and South the seven. Reading his partner's two as a distributional signal showing an odd number of cards in the suit, West realized that there was not likely to be another trick in hearts for the defense. The only other card that might provide the setting trick was the queen of clubs, which could assume real significance only if the diamond suit could be immobilized.

West therefore switched to a diamond at trick two. Winning in dummy with the ten, the declarer took a losing spade finesse to the queen. South won the next diamond with the ace as East completed an echo, and tried to steal a spade trick by leading the eight from hand. West was having none of that. He played the ace of spades and led his third diamond, finally cutting the link between the two hands.

The complete deal:

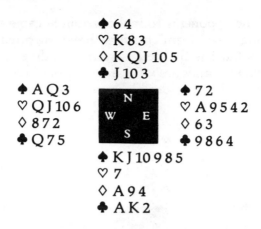

```
                    ♠ 6 4
                    ♡ K 8 3
                    ◇ K Q J 10 5
                    ♣ J 10 3
  ♠ A Q 3                          ♠ 7 2
  ♡ Q J 10 6        N              ♡ A 9 5 4 2
  ◇ 8 7 2       W       E          ◇ 6 3
  ♣ Q 7 5           S              ♣ 9 8 6 4
                    ♠ K J 10 9 8 5
                    ♡ 7
                    ◇ A 9 4
                    ♣ A K 2
```

Since West still had a small trump, the declarer could make no further use of dummy's diamond suit. He had to fall back on the club finesse, and when this failed so did the contract. Unlucky!

Note that if West continues with a heart at trick two declarer can make his contract in comfort by playing trumps from his own hand.

MAXIM. Sometimes you can score your own winners only by preventing declarer from scoring his.

---

31. GAME BOTH WAYS

Allowing the opponents to make a double game swing is the sort of thing that team players have nightmares about. Aggressive bidding is the best way of avoiding such a catastrophe. When the hands are wild and distributional, it is usually wise to bid on rather than double in a competitive situation.

Here is a case in point.

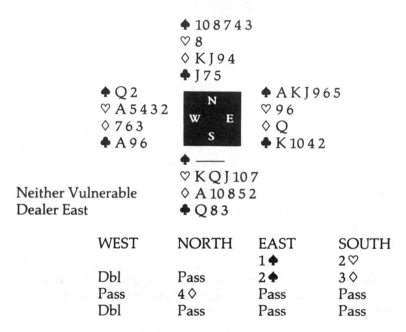

```
                    ♠ 10 8 7 4 3
                    ♡ 8
                    ◇ K J 9 4
                    ♣ J 7 5
    ♠ Q 2                            ♠ A K J 9 6 5
    ♡ A 5 4 3 2          N           ♡ 9 6
    ◇ 7 6 3          W       E       ◇ Q
    ♣ A 9 6              S           ♣ K 10 4 2
                    ♠ ──
                    ♡ K Q J 10 7
                    ◇ A 10 8 5 2
                    ♣ Q 8 3
```

Neither Vulnerable
Dealer East

WEST	NORTH	EAST	SOUTH
		1♠	2♡
Dbl	Pass	2♠	3◇
Pass	4◇	Pass	Pass
Dbl	Pass	Pass	Pass

West seemed determined to extract a penalty in one way or another, but he was soon regretting his final double. Playing in four diamonds South had no difficulty in making ten tricks for a score of 510.

In the other room North and South also bid up to four diamonds, but instead of doubling West pushed on to four spades. North doubled confidently and the defense started with two rounds of diamonds.

East was a careful player and did not make the mistake of trying to draw trumps. Ruffing the second diamond, he played a heart to dummy's ace and ruffed another diamond. The ace and king of clubs were cashed, and the play of a third club left the defenders without resource. The declarer's tenth trick came from a ruff of the thirteenth club with dummy's queen of spades.

That was 590 points to East-West and a total swing of 1100. Once again, North was too quick on the trigger with his double. In spite of the trump length he had no real defense against four spades and would have been advised to have taken the cheap sacrifice in five diamonds.

MAXIM. In high-level competitive situations, bidding on is less risky than doubling.

---

32. MEANS OF ACCESS

Contracts are frequently lost because declarer does not take enough trouble with his entries. It is vital to consider at the beginning which hand will need the entries later in the play. Here is an example:

♠ Q J 9 5 3
♡ K Q
♢ K J 9 4
♣ 7 2

```
      N
   W     E
      S
```

♠ K 10
♡ A 5
♢ Q 5 3 2
♣ A K Q 8 3

Both Vulnerable
Dealer South

SOUTH	WEST	NORTH	EAST
1♣	Pass	1♠	Pass
2 NT	Pass	3 NT	Pass
Pass	Pass		

West led the jack of hearts and the declarer assessed his chances. With five immediate winners he needed to develop four more, and he rightly decided that the spade suit offered the best chance. Winning the first trick with the queen of hearts, he played a low spade to his king which won the trick.

Belatedly South realized that if he played another spade to knock out the ace he would have no quick entry to the table, and the enemy might score three hearts and two aces. Still, he had a spade trick in the bag and the diamond suit might provide three more tricks. At trick three he played a low diamond to the jack. East took the ace and knocked out the ace of hearts, and when South continued with the queen of diamonds West showed out. The clubs failed to break, and South found he could no longer make the game.

The complete deal:

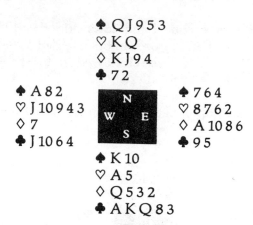

♠ Q J 9 5 3
♡ K Q
◇ K J 9 4
♣ 7 2

♠ A 8 2
♡ J 10 9 4 3
◇ 7
♣ J 10 6 4

♠ 7 6 4
♡ 8 7 6 2
◇ A 10 8 6
♣ 9 5

♠ K 10
♡ A 5
◇ Q 5 3 2
♣ A K Q 8 3

South's difficulties were all of his own making. Having decided that spades was the suit to establish, he should have made certain of a card of entry to the suit once the ace had been knocked out. All he had to do was to overtake the queen of hearts with his ace at trick one. The king of spades is then followed by the ten of spades. If West declines to take his ace on the second round, declarer has a choice of winning plays. He can either overtake in dummy and continue spades, or he can switch to diamonds. In either case he is assured of nine tricks.

MAXIM.	When you can win in either hand, preserve the winner in the hand that will need a later card of entry.

33. BEWARE OF PARROT-CRIES

Slogans such as 'second-hand low,' 'third-hand high' and 'cover an honor with an honor' can be regarded as good general guidelines but should not be followed slavishly. There are plenty of exceptions to such rules.

Note the deadly defense on this hand from a European Championship encounter between Denmark and Norway.

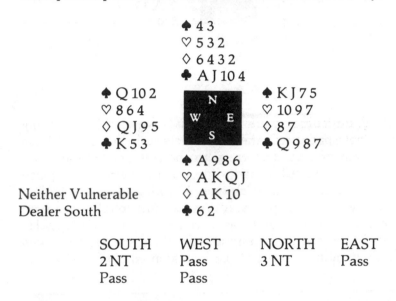

```
                    ♠ 4 3
                    ♡ 5 3 2
                    ◇ 6 4 3 2
                    ♣ A J 10 4
    ♠ Q 10 2                      ♠ K J 7 5
    ♡ 8 6 4          N            ♡ 10 9 7
    ◇ Q J 9 5     W     E         ◇ 8 7
    ♣ K 5 3          S            ♣ Q 9 8 7
                    ♠ A 9 8 6
                    ♡ A K Q J
Neither Vulnerable  ◇ A K 10
Dealer South        ♣ 6 2
```

SOUTH	WEST	NORTH	EAST
2 NT	Pass	3 NT	Pass
Pass	Pass		

West led the queen of diamonds against this routine contract of three notrump. With seven top tricks in his own hand, the Danish declarer needed two tricks in clubs for his contract. After winning the first trick with the king of diamonds he at once played the two of clubs, intending to finesse dummy's ten.

But the Norwegian West had been there before and put up the king of clubs — a play that could lose only if his partner had a singleton queen.

The appearance of the club king created a severe entry problem for the declarer. Realizing that he could not hope to score a second club trick unless West had the queen as well as the king, South played low from dummy on the first round. West promptly led a second club and the declarer tried for his contract by finessing the ten. When East produced the queen of clubs and returned a diamond, the declarer found himself unable to make more than seven tricks.

In the other room the play followed an identical course card for card, which gives some indication of the high general standard of play and defense.

Be sure to appreciate that the contract would have been made in comfort against a defender who refused to depart from the principle of 'second-hand low.'

MAXIM.   Beware of all slogans, including this one.

---

34. CUTTING THE LINK

Players often go astray in defense through getting their priorities the wrong way around. A cool, objective look at the situation will usually indicate which job ought to be tackled first.

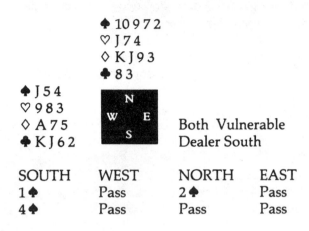

♠ 10 9 7 2
♡ J 7 4
◇ K J 9 3
♣ 8 3

♠ J 5 4
♡ 9 8 3
◇ A 7 5
♣ K J 6 2

Both Vulnerable
Dealer South

SOUTH	WEST	NORTH	EAST
1♠	Pass	2♠	Pass
4♠	Pass	Pass	Pass

West led the two of clubs on which East played the ace and South the five. East returned the four of clubs to the nine and jack. How should West continue?

The defenders had two club tricks in the bag and could count on the ace of diamonds as a third. Except in the unlikely event of the jack of spades proving to be a trick, West considered that the best chance of a further trick for the defense must lie in the heart suit. Accordingly he switched to the nine of hearts at trick three.

This defense was not good enough, however, for the full deal was as follows:

74

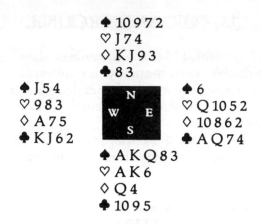

```
                    ♠ 10 9 7 2
                    ♡ J 7 4
                    ♢ K J 9 3
                    ♣ 8 3
    ♠ J 5 4          ┌─────────┐         ♠ 6
    ♡ 9 8 3          │    N    │         ♡ Q 10 5 2
    ♢ A 7 5          │  W   E  │         ♢ 10 8 6 2
    ♣ K J 6 2        │    S    │         ♣ A Q 7 4
                    └─────────┘
                    ♠ A K Q 8 3
                    ♡ A K 6
                    ♢ Q 4
                    ♣ 10 9 5
```

South won the king of hearts, drew trumps and played the queen of diamonds, rendering West helpless. Whether he won or ducked, South could eventually discard his losing heart on one of dummy's diamonds.

The defenders must hope for a trick in hearts, it is true, but there is no pressing need to attack the suit. The urgent task is to remove an entry from dummy. West knows from his partner's return of the four of clubs that South has a third card in the suit, and he should continue with the king of clubs at trick three, forcing dummy to ruff.

After drawing trumps South plays the queen of diamonds as before, but West holds up his ace. East starts an echo with the eight to show an even number of cards, and West knows to take his ace on the second round. Now West can switch to a heart, or simply play his fourth club. The declarer has been cut adrift from his diamond winners in dummy and must eventually lose a heart trick.

MAXIM.	Look for a chance to cut the link between declarer and dummy.

35. TOIL AND TROUBLE

When the opponents bid freely to game or slam it is generally a mistake to double, even though you may expect the contract to go down. Control your aggressive instincts and be satisfied to collect 50 or 100, for the danger of incurring a large minus score is ever present.

The worst doubles are those that provide the declarer with a clue to the winning line of play. Look at what happened on this hand.

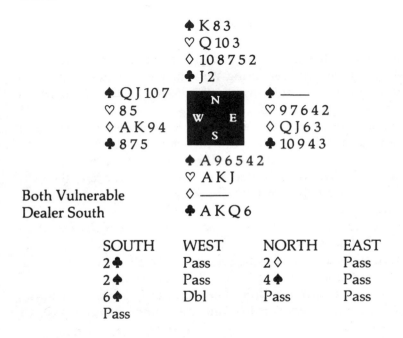

```
                        ♠ K 8 3
                        ♡ Q 10 3
                        ◊ 10 8 7 5 2
                        ♣ J 2
        ♠ Q J 10 7           N              ♠ ——
        ♡ 8 5                              ♡ 9 7 6 4 2
        ◊ A K 9 4       W       E          ◊ Q J 6 3
        ♣ 8 7 5              S              ♣ 10 9 4 3
                        ♠ A 9 6 5 4 2
                        ♡ A K J
Both Vulnerable         ◊ ——
Dealer South            ♣ A K Q 6
```

SOUTH	WEST	NORTH	EAST
2♣	Pass	2◊	Pass
2♠	Pass	4♠	Pass
6♠	Dbl	Pass	Pass
Pass			

West thought he was on firm enough ground when he doubled, but he began to feel uneasy when South ruffed the opening lead of the ace of diamonds. Taking the view that West was likely to have all the missing trumps, South did not make the normal play of a spade to dummy's king at trick two. Instead he played his low club to dummy's jack and ruffed a second diamond. The jack of hearts was overtaken with dummy's queen and a third diamond was ruffed.

South cashed the ace of hearts and continued with two top clubs, discarding the last heart from the table. Next came the

76

king of hearts, ruffed by West with the queen of spades and over-ruffed with dummy's king. After ruffing a fourth diamond in hand, South played the queen of clubs in this position:

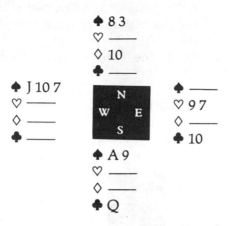

```
              ♠ 8 3
              ♡ —
              ◇ 10
              ♣ —
  ♠ J 10 7              ♠ —
  ♡ —                   ♡ 9 7
  ◇ —                   ◇ —
  ♣ —                   ♣ 10
              ♠ A 9
              ♡ —
              ◇ —
              ♣ Q
```

West had the choice of ruffing low and allowing an over-ruff in dummy, or ruffing high and conceding the last two tricks on his return.

It is true that a passive heart or club lead would have defeated the slam, but a double that needs to be followed up by double-dummy defense is a bad double. Without the giveaway double, South would have played a trump at trick two and the slam would have gone one down. That would have been 100 to East-West instead of 1660 to North-South.

MAXIM.   **Don't double freely-bid games or slams.**

77

36. PAR FOR THE COURSE

Bridge is the sort of game in which it is dangerous to judge by results. A mistake by the declarer is often cancelled out by a defensive error, and the par result may be achieved in spite of the worst efforts of both sides.

Here is an example of the kind of thing that is always happening.

```
              ♠ K 6 5
              ♡ 9 4 3
              ◊ A Q J 9 4
              ♣ 8 3
                    N
               W         E
                    S
              ♠ A Q 3
              ♡ A 10 7 2
              ◊ 6 2
              ♣ A K 6 4
```

Both Vulnerable
Dealer South

SOUTH	WEST	NORTH	EAST
1 NT	Pass	3 NT	Pass
Pass	Pass		

The opening lead of the ten of spades was won by the queen and South played a diamond to the jack and king. East continued the spade attack, South winning with the ace and persevering with diamonds. The diamonds divided 4-2, but after conceding a second trick in the suit to East the declarer had no difficulty in making his nine tricks, scoring three spades, three diamonds, two clubs and the ace of hearts.

The complete deal:

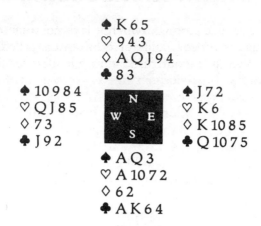

```
              ♠ K 6 5
              ♥ 9 4 3
              ◇ A Q J 9 4
              ♣ 8 3
♠ 10 9 8 4         N          ♠ J 7 2
♥ Q J 8 5       W     E       ♥ K 6
◇ 7 3              S          ◇ K 10 8 5
♣ J 9 2                       ♣ Q 10 7 5
              ♠ A Q 3
              ♥ A 10 7 2
              ◇ 6 2
              ♣ A K 6 4
```

Better play by East would have led to the defeat of the game. If East declines to take his king of diamonds on the first round, the declarer is unable to establish a third trick in the suit for lack of entries. Failure to hold up in such situations is a common defensive error.

But South should not have given East the chance to hold up. Since he can afford to lose two tricks in diamonds he should insert the nine from dummy on the first round. This could draw the king, but even if not it compels the defenders to use up one of their stoppers at a time when dummy still retains a card of entry in the suit. East wins with the ten and continues spades (as good as anything), but South wins with the ace and plays his second diamond to the jack. Whether East takes his king immediately or not, South is able to force out the last defensive stopper and make sure of nine tricks.

MAXIM.   Remember that a duck can forestall an enemy hold-up.

79

37. IDIOT'S LEAD?

An expert friend of mine, over-reacting to some disaster in the distant past, habitually refers to the lead of a trump as 'the idiot's lead.' Well, as a confirmed trump leader of many years' standing I would like to offer some encouragement to fellow-idiots.

There are several situations where a trump lead is marked, the most obvious being when the opponents bid high on values that are mainly distributional. In the 1967 European Championships at Dublin the Irish created some sort of record in their match against Poland by bidding a slam of a combined total of 12 high-card points. Here is the hand.

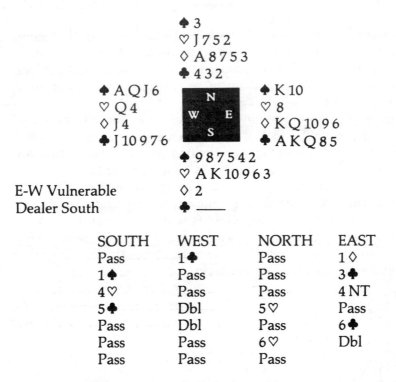

```
                    ♠ 3
                    ♡ J 7 5 2
                    ◇ A 8 7 5 3
                    ♣ 4 3 2
     ♠ A Q J 6              ♠ K 10
     ♡ Q 4                  ♡ 8
     ◇ J 4                  ◇ K Q 10 9 6
     ♣ J 10 9 7 6          ♣ A K Q 8 5
                    ♠ 9 8 7 5 4 2
                    ♡ A K 10 9 6 3
E-W Vulnerable      ◇ 2
Dealer South        ♣ ——
```

SOUTH	WEST	NORTH	EAST
Pass	1♣	Pass	1◇
1♠	Pass	Pass	3♣
4♡	Pass	Pass	4 NT
5♣	Dbl	5♡	Pass
Pass	Dbl	Pass	6♣
Pass	Pass	6♡	Dbl
Pass	Pass	Pass	

West led the jack of diamonds to dummy's ace, and at trick two a spade was won by East with the ten. After ruffing the club return, South was able to establish the spade suit by ruffing three times in dummy, thus making his doubled slam for a score of 1210.

That initial diamond lead is hard to understand, for West knew that the defenders had all three side suits buttoned up. The four of hearts should have hit the table before the echo of the final pass had died away. Naturally West has to follow up by making sure that he wins the first round of spades in order to lead his second trump.

In the other room the Poles made the same twelve tricks in five hearts doubled for a score of 750. The Irish thus gained 10 IMP's where they might have lost 13.

MAXIM.	Lead a trump when opponents bid high on distributional values and you have strength in the other three suits.

38. THE DANGER HAND

When there is a possibility of losing the lead twice in developing the tricks needed for the contract, declarer has to give some thought to the problem of which entry to attack first. The right choice is the entry that may lie in the danger hand — that is the hand containing the long suit.

Neither declarer got it right on this hand from a team game.

$$\spadesuit\ 7\ 3$$
$$\heartsuit\ 6\ 5$$
$$\diamondsuit\ A\ Q\ J\ 8\ 4$$
$$\clubsuit\ A\ 6\ 5\ 3$$

```
        N
    W       E
        S
```

Both Vulnerable
Dealer South

$$\spadesuit\ A\ K\ 6$$
$$\heartsuit\ K\ Q\ 9\ 2$$
$$\diamondsuit\ 10\ 9\ 5\ 2$$
$$\clubsuit\ K\ 4$$

SOUTH	WEST	NORTH	EAST
1 NT	Pass	3 NT	Pass
Pass	Pass		

West led the jack of clubs, and in the first room the declarer saw that he would have more than enough tricks if the diamond finesse worked. He played low from dummy and captured East's queen of clubs with his king. The diamond ten was played for a finesse, but East produced the king and returned a club to dummy's ace. After running the diamonds South had to try for his ninth trick in hearts, but West took the ace and cashed three clubs to put the contract one down.

The complete deal:

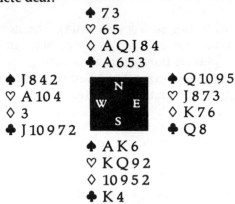

```
                    ♠ 7 3
                    ♡ 6 5
                    ◊ A Q J 8 4
                    ♣ A 6 5 3
    ♠ J 8 4 2          N          ♠ Q 10 9 5
    ♡ A 10 4       W       E      ♡ J 8 7 3
    ◊ 3                S          ◊ K 7 6
    ♣ J 10 9 7 2                  ♣ Q 8
                    ♠ A K 6
                    ♡ K Q 9 2
                    ◊ 10 9 5 2
                    ♣ K 4
```

In the other room the declarer was aware of the danger of a
5-2 club break and tried to overcome it by ducking the first
trick. Alas, he had overlooked another danger. When the queen
of clubs was allowed to win East switched smartly to the ten of
spades, and the defenders could not be prevented from scoring
two spades to go with their heart, their diamond and their
club.

Holding up is not the answer on this type of hand. Declarer
must win and attack the entry that may lie in the hand
containing the long suit. The correct play is to win the first trick
in dummy with the ace of clubs and play a heart to the king.
West may win the ace, but there is no distribution that allows
the defenders to score more than three heart tricks. And if West
returns a club, South can finesse the diamonds in comfort,
knowing that if the finesse loses and East returns a club the suit
is breaking no worse than 4-3.

MAXIM.   Attack first the entry that may be held by the
defender with the long suit.

---

39. NIGHTMARE

Missing a slam is not so very unusual, but going down in three notrump when there is a cold grand slam in a suit is the sort of thing that players have nightmares about. It happened in a team game and the pair concerned had to listen, red-faced, to some harsh words from their team-mates.

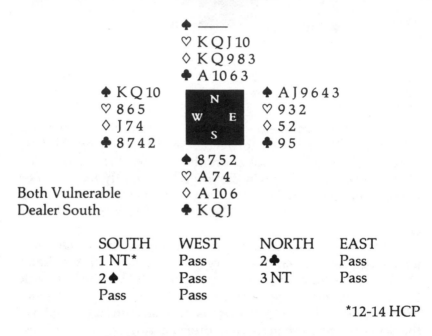

♠ ——
♡ K Q J 10
◊ K Q 9 8 3
♣ A 10 6 3

♠ K Q 10
♡ 8 6 5
◊ J 7 4
♣ 8 7 4 2

♠ A J 9 6 4 3
♡ 9 3 2
◊ 5 2
♣ 9 5

♠ 8 7 5 2
♡ A 7 4
◊ A 10 6
♣ K Q J

Both Vulnerable
Dealer South

SOUTH	WEST	NORTH	EAST
1 NT*	Pass	2♣	Pass
2♠	Pass	3 NT	Pass
Pass	Pass		

*12-14 HCP

North was hoping to hear a heart bid from his partner. When the spade bid came instead, he made the too-hasty decision to play in three notrump.

In spite of the spade bid, West chose the king of spades as his opening lead, striking oil in his partner's hand. East signaled joyfully with the nine, and the defenders took the first six tricks to put the contract two down.

84

In the other room:

SOUTH	WEST	NORTH	EAST
1 NT	Pass	2♣	Pass
2♠	Pass	3◊	Pass
3♡	Pass	4♣	Pass
4◊	Pass	4♠	Pass
5♣	Pass	5♡	Pass
6♣	Pass	7◊	Pass
Pass	Pass		

The auction started in a similar way, but North did not assume that three notrump would be the right spot. He bid a natural three diamonds on the second round, knowing that he could always settle for three notrump if partner bid it or rebid his spades.

In practice South had a suitable hand for playing in diamonds, and a series of cue bids pin-pointed all the key cards. At the end North was able to bid the grand slam in diamonds with a fair degree of confidence.

There was no defeating the grand slam and the total swing on the hand was 2340 aggregate points or 20 IMP's.

MAXIM. Four cards do not always add up to a stopper.

---

40. OPPORTUNITY KNOCKS

Close partnership co-operation is often needed in order to exploit opportunities in defense. On the following hand one defender was on his toes but the other fell asleep at the critical moment.

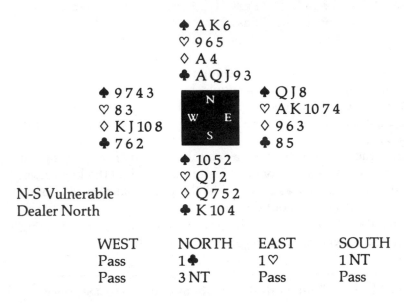

```
                   ♠ A K 6
                   ♡ 9 6 5
                   ◊ A 4
                   ♣ A Q J 9 3
        ♠ 9 7 4 3              ♠ Q J 8
        ♡ 8 3                  ♡ A K 10 7 4
        ◊ K J 10 8             ◊ 9 6 3
        ♣ 7 6 2                ♣ 8 5
                   ♠ 10 5 2
                   ♡ Q J 2
N-S Vulnerable     ◊ Q 7 5 2
Dealer North       ♣ K 10 4
```

WEST	NORTH	EAST	SOUTH
Pass	1♣	1♡	1 NT
Pass	3 NT	Pass	Pass

West led the eight of hearts and East paused to take stock. South was sure to have at least one of the minor-suit kings, in which case it would not do to let him score a heart trick. That would enable him to run at least nine tricks, by finessing in clubs if necessary.

Realizing that the defensive hopes rested with the diamonds, East won the first trick with the king of hearts and switched to the six of diamonds. This was covered by the seven and eight, and the trick was won by the ace. The declarer ran his five club tricks, East discarding hearts while South and West shed spades. Then came a second heart to the ace. East returned the nine of diamonds, but West had to overtake with the ten and the defense could make no more than four tricks.

It should have been clear to West that there would be difficulty in scoring the three diamond tricks needed to defeat the contract if he kept all his honor cards. He had the chance to shine by unblocking the ten of diamonds on the first round. Then he would have been able to throw the eight under his partner's nine on the second round, leaving the lead in the right hand.

MAXIM.   Unblock your high cards to facilitate com-
          munications.

---

41. WHEN ENTRIES ARE SHORT

Establishing a long suit can be a tricky business when dummy is short of entries, and the right play is not always obvious. The declarer discovered a gap in his technique on the following hand.

```
              ♠ K 6 4
              ♡ 9 5
              ◊ 7 6 2
              ♣ K J 6 5 3
                 ┌─────┐
                 │  N  │
                 │ W E │
                 │  S  │
                 └─────┘
              ♠ A 7 2
              ♡ A K 8 6
              ◊ A K 9
              ♣ Q 4 2
```

Both Vulnerable
Dealer South

SOUTH	WEST	NORTH	EAST
2 NT	Pass	3 NT	Pass
Pass	Pass		

West led the three of spades, and South correctly played low in dummy in order to preserve the king as a later entry. Capturing East's jack with the ace, South played a low club towards dummy. West played low and the jack won the trick, but East showed out when a second club was played from the table. West played his ace on South's queen and continued with the spade attack, removing the outside entry from dummy. Declarer was thus unable to make more than two tricks in clubs and the contract eventually went one down.

The complete deal:

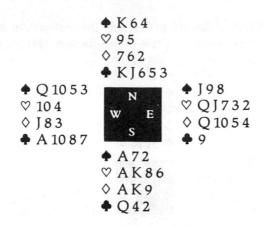

```
                    ♠ K 6 4
                    ♡ 9 5
                    ◊ 7 6 2
                    ♣ K J 6 5 3
  ♠ Q 10 5 3          N          ♠ J 9 8
  ♡ 10 4        W          E      ♡ Q J 7 3 2
  ◊ J 8 3            S          ◊ Q 10 5 4
  ♣ A 10 8 7                     ♣ 9
                    ♠ A 7 2
                    ♡ A K 8 6
                    ◊ A K 9
                    ♣ Q 4 2
```

South should have analyzed the situation more closely. The spades appeared to be 4-3, which meant that South could afford to lose two club tricks in order to score three. The contract would clearly be made with an overtrick on a normal 3-2 club break, and South should have directed his mind to the possibility of a 4-1 split.

On a non-spade lead it would have been possible to cope with a 4-1 club break by playing low from both hands on the first round of clubs. This does not work once spades have been attacked, for on winning the first club the defenders simply knock out the spade king and then hold up the club ace until the third round. After a spade lead the contract cannot be made if East has four clubs headed by the ace, but if West has four clubs it can be made by playing the queen of clubs at trick two. This forces West to take his ace immediately (otherwise South scores the club tricks he needs by leading twice toward the king and the jack). With the club ace gone, South wins the spade return and ducks a club, thereby ensuring three club tricks.

MAXIM.	Force out an enemy stopper on the first round.

42. DIAGNOSING THE RUFF

There are many hands on which the defenders can prevail only if they exercise a little imagination. Here is a fairly common situation.

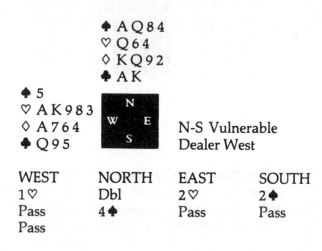

♠ A Q 8 4
♡ Q 6 4
◇ K Q 9 2
♣ A K

♠ 5
♡ A K 9 8 3
◇ A 7 6 4
♣ Q 9 5

N-S Vulnerable
Dealer West

WEST	NORTH	EAST	SOUTH
1♡	Dbl	2♡	2♠
Pass	4♠	Pass	Pass
Pass			

West began with the ace of hearts on which East contributed the jack and South the five. How should West continue?

East's jack of hearts was taken to indicate four cards in the suit, which meant there was no chance of a second heart trick. West realized that the contract would be defeated only if the defenders could score two tricks in trumps. On the bidding it seemed unlikely that East would have two trump tricks in his own right, but there was another possibility. If East had the king of spades plus a doubleton diamond, it should be possible to achieve a diamond ruff.

To prepare the ground for this, West switched to the four of diamonds at trick two.

The complete deal:

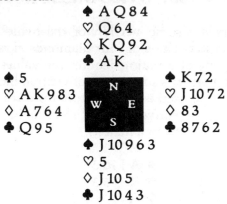

```
                  ♠ A Q 8 4
                  ♡ Q 6 4
                  ◇ K Q 9 2
                  ♣ A K
♠ 5                              ♠ K 7 2
♡ A K 9 8 3          N           ♡ J 10 7 2
◇ A 7 6 4        W     E         ◇ 8 3
♣ Q 9 5             S            ♣ 8 7 6 2
                  ♠ J 10 9 6 3
                  ♡ 5
                  ◇ J 10 5
                  ♣ J 10 4 3
```

The declarer won the diamond switch in hand and ran the jack of spades. East won the king, returned his second diamond to the ace and ruffed the diamond continuation to put the contract one down.

The declarer might have tried to avoid the ruff by rejecting the trump finesse, playing the ace and another spade instead, but this would have done him no good on the actual lie of the cards.

MAXIM.   Look out for the chance of giving partner a ruff.

---

43. SWISS MISS

Many players use some version of the Swiss Convention, whereby a bid of four clubs or four diamonds in response to an opening bid of one of a major denotes the values for a strong raise to game in partner's suit. This convention has great merits but it should not be used as a substitute for a forcing takeout. Misapplication of the convention led to an unhappy result for one team on this hand from a match.

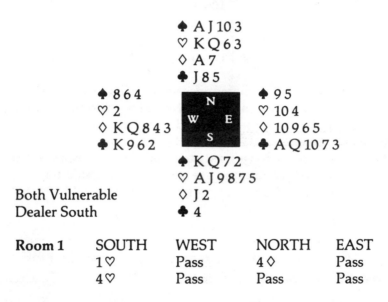

```
                          ♠ A J 10 3
                          ♡ K Q 6 3
                          ◇ A 7
                          ♣ J 8 5
        ♠ 8 6 4                         ♠ 9 5
        ♡ 2              N              ♡ 10 4
        ◇ K Q 8 4 3    W   E            ◇ 10 9 6 5
        ♣ K 9 6 2        S              ♣ A Q 10 7 3
                          ♠ K Q 7 2
                          ♡ A J 9 8 7 5
Both Vulnerable           ◇ J 2
Dealer South              ♣ 4
```

Room 1	SOUTH	WEST	NORTH	EAST
	1♡	Pass	4◇	Pass
	4♡	Pass	Pass	Pass

North's jump to four diamonds affirmed good heart support along with two aces. Reasoning that even if the trumps were solid there were likely to be two losers in the side suits, South signed off in four hearts. He was absolutely right to sign off, since there were no more than eleven tricks to be made in hearts.

Room 2	SOUTH	WEST	NORTH	EAST
	1♡	Pass	2♣	Pass
	4♣	Pass	5◇	Pass
	6♣	Pass	Pass	Pass

In the other room North properly considered his hand to be

worth a full-blooded forcing takeout of two spades, which South raised to four. The double raise in a forcing situation is used to indicate excellent trump support along with minimal values.

North had intended to support hearts on the second round but now changed his mind. It was clear that the hand could well play better in spades since the losing diamond could be discarded on partner's long hearts. North therefore cue-bid the ace of diamonds and South bid the slam on the strength of his singleton club.

There was nothing much in the play. On a diamond lead North was unable to negotiate a club ruff but had to draw trumps, relying on a 3-2 break. This duly materialized and his team gained 13 IMP's.

MAXIM.   Don't send a boy to do a man's job.

---

44. AN EAR TO THE BIDDING

It is remarkable how often the fate of a slam contract depends on the choice of opening lead. The sensible course for the defender on lead is to carry out a careful review of the bidding before deciding on the best shot.

Missing the killing lead proved expensive on this hand from a Gold Cup match.

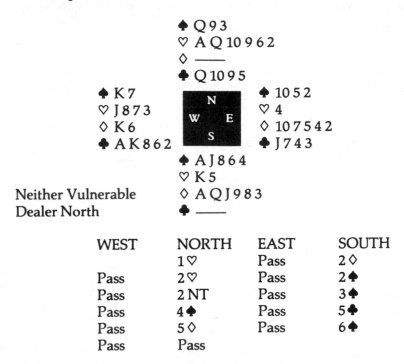

♠ Q 9 3
♡ A Q 10 9 6 2
◇ ——
♣ Q 10 9 5

♠ K 7
♡ J 8 7 3
◇ K 6
♣ A K 8 6 2

♠ 10 5 2
♡ 4
◇ 10 7 5 4 2
♣ J 7 4 3

♠ A J 8 6 4
♡ K 5
◇ A Q J 9 8 3
♣ ——

Neither Vulnerable
Dealer North

WEST	NORTH	EAST	SOUTH
	1♡	Pass	2◇
Pass	2♡	Pass	2♠
Pass	2 NT	Pass	3♠
Pass	4♠	Pass	5♣
Pass	5◇	Pass	6♠
Pass	Pass		

Although not expecting the slam to be made, West chose not to double, which was just as well in view of his choice of lead — the king of clubs. South ruffed in hand, ruffed a small diamond in dummy, and ran the queen of spades to the king. West returned his trump and the declarer drew a third round.

Avoiding the trap of testing the hearts prematurely, South cashed the ace of diamonds and received a bonus when the king fell. On the queen and jack of diamonds West discarded the remaining small clubs, but the play of the last trump turned the screw. Unable to keep four hearts and the ace of clubs, West had to surrender.

The hand was well played, but the declarer would have no chance if West had listened more carefully to the bidding before selecting his opening lead. He could hardly expect to score a club trick, since South had announced a void in the suit with his cue bid.

It takes a heart lead to kill the slam, and this should not have been to difficult for West to find. On the bidding South was marked with a 5-2-6-0 shape, and West had only to envision six hearts on his left to see the possibility of giving his partner a ruff.

MAXIM.	Review the bidding before choosing an opening lead.

45. BLOCK IT!

A well-known rule of thumb offers guidance on the subject of holding up an ace at notrump. With five cards in the enemy suit hold up the ace twice, with six cards hold up once, and with seven cards don't bother to hold up at all. The rules are designed to take care of the dangerous situation where one defender has five cards in the suit.

But there are hands on which hold-up play has to be abandoned in favor of a different technique. Here is an example.

```
            ♠ K 4
            ♡ A 10 3
            ◊ Q 10 9 5
            ♣ J 6 5 2

                 N
              W     E
                 S

            ♠ A Q 7
            ♡ 6 5 4
            ◊ K J 7 2
            ♣ A K 3
```

Both Vulnerable
Dealer South

SOUTH	WEST	NORTH	EAST
1 NT	Pass	3 NT	Pass
Pass	Pass		

West led the queen of hearts and the declarer saw that he was safe for nine tricks as long as the defenders could be prevented from scoring four tricks in hearts. With six cards in the enemy suit the rule said to hold up once, so South held off the first trick but took the ace of hearts on the second round. Then he played on diamonds, hoping that if West had five hearts the ace of diamonds would be with East. He was out of luck.

The full hand:

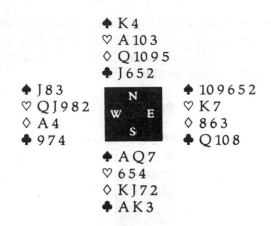

```
                    ♠ K 4
                    ♡ A 10 3
                    ◊ Q 10 9 5
                    ♣ J 6 5 2
  ♠ J 8 3                         ♠ 10 9 6 5 2
  ♡ Q J 9 8 2         N           ♡ K 7
  ◊ A 4          W         E      ◊ 8 6 3
  ♣ 9 7 4            S             ♣ Q 10 8
                    ♠ A Q 7
                    ♡ 6 5 4
                    ◊ K J 7 2
                    ♣ A K 3
```

West produced the ace of diamonds and took three more heart tricks to defeat the contract.

A more experienced declarer would have realized that the opening lead of the heart queen combined with the presence of the ten in dummy offered a superior way of guarding against a 5-2 break in the suit. If the hearts were 5-2, East's king must be doubleton and he would be caught in a cruel dilemma if South played the ace of hearts on the first trick. If he keeps the heart king, the suit is blocked and South can knock out the ace of diamonds without fear. Alternatively, if East unblocks the king of hearts under the ace, the ten of hearts in dummy serves as a second stopper in the suit. Either way South makes his contract without difficulty.

MAXIM.   Scorn the hold-up when you can block the suit by winning the trick.

---

46. UNBLOCK IT!

Sometimes it takes a little foresight to make sure that the required entries will be available at the right time. The declarer slipped up on the following hand, but it is doubtful if many players would have done better.

```
              ♠ Q 5
              ♡ 9 8 5 3
              ◊ A K Q 10 7
              ♣ J 4
                   N
                W     E
                   S
              ♠ A 7 2
              ♡ A Q J
E-W Vulnerable    ◊ J 4 3
Dealer South      ♣ A K 8 5
```

SOUTH	WEST	NORTH	EAST
1♣	Pass	1◊	Pass
3 NT	Pass	4 NT	Pass
6 NT	Pass	Pass	Pass

North added on a point or two for his good suit and South did the same for his good controls, the result being an ambitious slam. West led the jack of spades which boded no good for declarer. South tried the queen from dummy, but East produced the king and was allowed to hold the trick. Winning the spade return, South played a small diamond to dummy's ten, hoping to score nine tricks in the red suits to put alongside his three in the blacks. His planning was not good enough, however, for the full hand turned out to be:

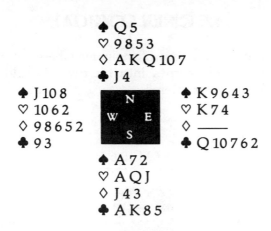

```
              ♠ Q 5
              ♡ 9 8 5 3
              ◊ A K Q 10 7
              ♣ J 4
  ♠ J 10 8              ♠ K 9 6 4 3
  ♡ 10 6 2             ♡ K 7 4
  ◊ 9 8 6 5 2          ◊ ———
  ♣ 9 3                ♣ Q 10 7 6 2
              ♠ A 7 2
              ♡ A Q J
              ◊ J 4 3
              ♣ A K 8 5
```

South needed three diamond entries in dummy in order to bring in the hearts (two entries to take heart finesses and one to cash the established long heart). Normally one would expect to have three entries anyway, for a 5-0 break occurs no more than one time in twenty-five deals. But the effect here was disastrous for declarer. The ten of diamonds was followed by a successful heart finesse and then the four of diamonds from hand. South hoped to be allowed to finesse the seven of diamonds, but West was having none of that. He inserted the eight of diamonds, forcing out dummy's queen and blocking the suit. South was able to establish the long heart all right, but he had to overtake the jack of diamonds with the king in order to cash it. He thus made only four diamonds and finished one trick short of his contract.

It is easy to see the right play after the event. South should play the jack of diamonds on the first round, overtaking with the queen when West follows suit. Now the 5-0 break poses no problem, for South can finesse twice against the nine and eight of diamonds, ensuring three entries to dummy without sacrificing a trick in the suit.

MAXIM. Unblock by overtaking when you can afford to do so.

---

47. ONLY LOGICAL

Defense is the department of the game where the player with a logical mind really comes into his own. Would you have solved this defensive problem?

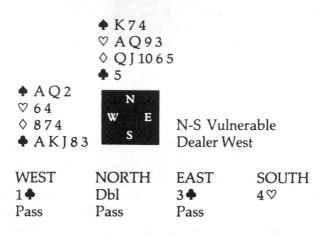

```
                        ♠ K74
                        ♡ AQ93
                        ♢ QJ1065
                        ♣ 5
        ♠ AQ2           N
        ♡ 64
        ♢ 874         W   E       N-S Vulnerable
        ♣ AKJ83         S         Dealer West
```

WEST	NORTH	EAST	SOUTH
1♣	Dbl	3♣	4♡
Pass	Pass	Pass	

West led the ace of clubs on which East played the two and South the four. How should he continue?

It is a matter of working out where the defensive tricks can come from. West knows that if the contract is to be defeated his partner will need to produce a trick in one of the red suits — either the king of hearts or the ace of diamonds. On the bidding East can hardly have both of these cards, and it follows that the other two defensive tricks must come from the spade suit. West can see that the spades will yield two tricks if his partner has either the jack or the ten and nine. The play that allows for both possibilites is a switch to the queen of spades at trick two.

West found the play of the queen of spades at trick two and was duly rewarded when the full hand turned out to be:

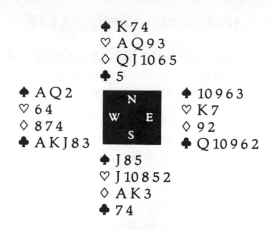

```
              ♠ K74
              ♡ AQ93
              ◇ QJ1065
              ♣ 5
♠ AQ2              N          ♠ 10963
♡ 64          W       E       ♡ K7
◇ 874             S          ◇ 92
♣ AKJ83                       ♣ Q10962
              ♠ J85
              ♡ J10852
              ◇ AK3
              ♣ 74
```

The deadly switch to the queen of spades is the sort of thing that looks like black magic to the uninitiated, but it is really just a matter of logic.

Dummy won the trick with the king, but when East came in with the king of hearts he was able to return the ten of spades to give the defenders two tricks in the suit.

MAXIM. Work out what partner needs to have to defeat the contract.

---

48. EGGS AND BASKETS

When planning the play of a hand it is desirable to keep open as many options as possible. A French declarer failed to do this is a European Championship match against Sweden a number of years ago.

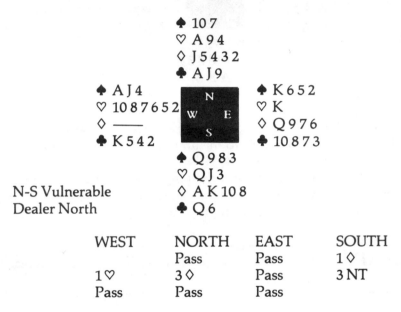

```
                    ♠ 10 7
                    ♡ A 9 4
                    ◇ J 5 4 3 2
                    ♣ A J 9
    ♠ A J 4                        ♠ K 6 5 2
    ♡ 10 8 7 6 5 2      N          ♡ K
    ◇ ─────         W     E        ◇ Q 9 7 6
    ♣ K 5 4 2          S           ♣ 10 8 7 3
                    ♠ Q 9 8 3
                    ♡ Q J 3
N-S Vulnerable      ◇ A K 10 8
Dealer North        ♣ Q 6
```

WEST	NORTH	EAST	SOUTH
	Pass	Pass	1 ◇
1 ♡	3 ◇	Pass	3 NT
Pass	Pass	Pass	

West led a small heart against three notrump. The double-dummy play is to put up the ace, but South could hardly be exepcted to find this. He played low from dummy and East won with the king. East switched to a spade and the defenders took their three tricks in the suit, the nine of clubs being thrown from dummy. A fourth spade was played to the queen, and South put all his eggs in the one basket when he discarded the jack of clubs from the table.

The play of the ace of diamonds exposed the bad break and the declarer realized with dismay that dummy was short of an entry to bring in the suit. Unable to make more than four tricks in diamonds, South was held to eight tricks altogether.

South should, of course, have discarded the nine of hearts on the fourth round of spades. When the diamonds proved awkward he could then have fallen back on the club finesse for his ninth trick.

In the other room West played in two hearts, going quietly two down for the loss of 100 points. France therefore lost 5 IMP's on a hand where they might have gained 11.

MAXIM. Try to leave yourself with something to fall back upon when the main chance fails.

---

49. PARTNER IS ON YOUR SIDE

Many defensive tragedies could be avoided if players would only school themselves to give a little more thought to their partners' problems. Here is a case in point.

```
                    ♠ A J 3
                    ♡ K Q 7 3
                    ◇ K J 6 2
                    ♣ A K
  ♠ 10 9 4            N
  ♡ 6              W     E
  ◇ A 10 9 3          S          Both Vulnerable
  ♣ J 9 6 5 2                    Dealer North
```

WEST	NORTH	EAST	SOUTH
	2 NT	Pass	3 ♡
Pass	4 ♣	Pass	4 ♡
Pass	Pass	Pass	

West led the ten of spades and the three was played from dummy. East won the trick with the king and returned the eight of diamonds on which the declarer played the four. West realized that his partner would need to have the ace of trumps if the contract was to be defeated. Placing East with a doubleton diamond, West ducked on the first round in order to preserve communications.

That turned out to be the wrong defense. The declarer knocked out the ace of trumps and was unable to lose more than three tricks, for the complete deal was as follows:

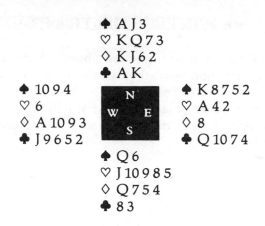

$\spadesuit$ A J 3
$\heartsuit$ K Q 7 3
$\diamond$ K J 6 2
$\clubsuit$ A K

$\spadesuit$ 10 9 4
$\heartsuit$ 6
$\diamond$ A 10 9 3
$\clubsuit$ J 9 6 5 2

$\spadesuit$ K 8 7 5 2
$\heartsuit$ A 4 2
$\diamond$ 8
$\clubsuit$ Q 10 7 4

$\spadesuit$ Q 6
$\heartsuit$ J 10 9 8 5
$\diamond$ Q 7 5 4
$\clubsuit$ 8 3

Clearly the contract would have been defeated if West had taken the ace of diamonds and returned the suit to give his partner a ruff.

Although it was West who looked foolish, he was really the victim of his partner's thoughtlessness. East's proper play is very simple. Knowing he needs to find his partner with the ace of diamonds, he should cash the ace of hearts before leading his singleton diamond. West would then have no option but to take his ace and return the suit.

It follows that when East fails to cash the ace of trumps West is right to duck the diamond, playing his partner for a doubleton.

MAXIM. Make life easy for partner, the guy on your side.

---

50. WRONG CONTRACT

There is a long-standing argument about which phase of the game is the more important, the bidding or the play. Without taking sides I shall merely observe that any player who consistently reaches sensible contracts has a big advantage.

Two experienced pairs missed the sensible contract on this hand from a team game.

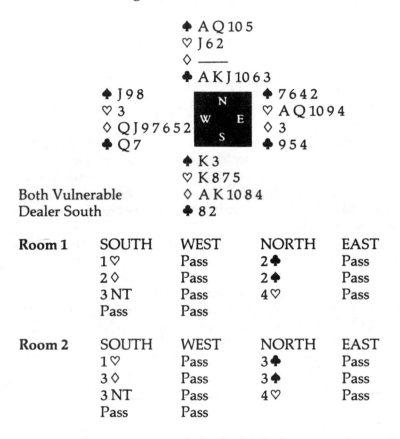

```
                      ♠ A Q 10 5
                      ♡ J 6 2
                      ◊ ——
                      ♣ A K J 10 6 3
         ♠ J 9 8                      ♠ 7 6 4 2
         ♡ 3             N            ♡ A Q 10 9 4
         ◊ Q J 9 7 6 5 2  W   E       ◊ 3
         ♣ Q 7            S           ♣ 9 5 4
                      ♠ K 3
                      ♡ K 8 7 5
Both Vulnerable       ◊ A K 10 8 4
Dealer South          ♣ 8 2
```

Room 1	SOUTH	WEST	NORTH	EAST
	1 ♡	Pass	2 ♣	Pass
	2 ◊	Pass	2 ♠	Pass
	3 NT	Pass	4 ♡	Pass
	Pass	Pass		

Room 2	SOUTH	WEST	NORTH	EAST
	1 ♡	Pass	3 ♣	Pass
	3 ◊	Pass	3 ♠	Pass
	3 NT	Pass	4 ♡	Pass
	Pass	Pass		

Winning the opening spade lead, the declarers tried to cash the ace and king of diamonds. East ruffed the second diamond and returned a spade, and the declarers had to lose three further trump tricks.

The sensible contract is, of course, three notrump. No fewer than twelve tricks can be made on the lie of the cards.

In both rooms North had the opportunity to allow his partner to play in notrump, but the real culprits were the South players who elected to open the bidding in that feeble heart suit. No doubt they were actuated by fear of missing a heart fit, but it is always a mistake to distort the bidding in this manner.

South should open one diamond and rebid the respectable diamond suit after a spade or a club response. If North cannot bid hearts at some stage, South should have no wish to play there.

MAXIM.	Don't distort the bidding by opening in a suit other than your longest and strongest.

51. SLEEPY DEFENSE

Players rarely go to sleep in the bidding, seldom nod off when playing the hand, but quite often take a little nap on defense. Yet there is no phase of the game where it is more important to remain alert. This is the sort of thing that is always happening.

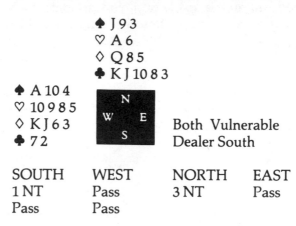

```
              ♠ J 9 3
              ♡ A 6
              ◇ Q 8 5
              ♣ K J 10 8 3
♠ A 10 4         N
♡ 10 9 8 5
◇ K J 6 3      W    E        Both Vulnerable
♣ 7 2           S           Dealer South
```

SOUTH	WEST	NORTH	EAST
1 NT	Pass	3 NT	Pass
Pass	Pass		

West led the ten of hearts to the six, queen and king. At trick two the declarer played a low spade, winning with dummy's jack when West played low. Two more heart tricks and five clubs quickly brought the declarer's tally up to nine tricks.

The complete deal:

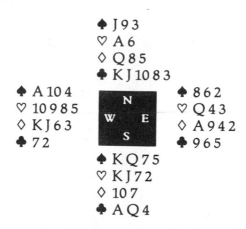

```
              ♠ J 9 3
              ♡ A 6
              ◇ Q 8 5
              ♣ K J 10 8 3
♠ A 10 4         N        ♠ 8 6 2
♡ 10 9 8 5               ♡ Q 4 3
◇ K J 6 3      W    E     ◇ A 9 4 2
♣ 7 2           S        ♣ 9 6 5
              ♠ K Q 7 5
              ♡ K J 7 2
              ◇ 10 7
              ♣ A Q 4
```

This sequence of events should have been anticipated. From

the play to the first trick West knows that declarer has three heart tricks, and South's failure to play on clubs is a strong indication that the suit is solid. It follows that declarer will make this contract if he is allowed to steal just one spade trick.

An alert defender would therefore go straight up with the ace of spades and switch to diamonds as the only remaining chance. Any diamond will not do. West needs to find his partner with either A 10 x or A 9 x x in the suit, and the card that caters to both possibilities is the jack of diamonds. Whether declarer covers with dummy's queen or not, the defenders can run four diamond tricks to put the contract one down.

MAXIM. Don't duck when this concedes the game-going trick.

52. SURPRISE, SURPRISE!

It does not pay to be too predictable at this game. When the bidding suggests that the declarer is likely to be well-prepared against the obvious line of attack, it will usually be a good idea to try something else.

This hand from an international trial caused problems throughout the field.

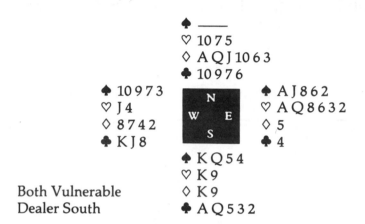

```
                    ♠ ——
                    ♡ 10 7 5
                    ◇ A Q J 10 6 3
                    ♣ 10 9 7 6
   ♠ 10 9 7 3                        ♠ A J 8 6 2
   ♡ J 4            N                ♡ A Q 8 6 3 2
   ◇ 8 7 4 2    W       E            ◇ 5
   ♣ K J 8          S                ♣ 4
                    ♠ K Q 5 4
                    ♡ K 9
                    ◇ K 9
                    ♣ A Q 5 3 2
```

Both Vulnerable
Dealer South

At most of the tables North and South played in one of their minor suits, those who reached the five-level being defeated by the unlucky club position. But at one table the bidding developed in a different way.

SOUTH	WEST	NORTH	EAST
1♣	Pass	1◇	Dbl
Redbl	1♠	3♠	Pass
3 NT	Pass	Pass	Pass

West led the ten of spades against the contract of three notrump. A heart was thrown from dummy, East put in the six and South won with the king. Playing the nine of diamonds to dummy's ten, declarer returned a club for a finesse of the queen. West won and continued spades, giving South his ninth trick.

There is no defense after the initial spade lead, and West might have suspected that this would be the case. Having contracted for three notrump in the face of his partner's

110

advertised spade void, South was likely to be well prepared for a lead in the suit. Reasoning on these lines, West might have tried his partner's second suit. The lead of the jack of hearts would, in fact, have left declarer a trick short.

MAXIM.   When declarer seems to be well prepared for the obvious lead, try something else.

53. PRESERVING AN OPTION

Most hands offer a choice between several different lines of play, some of which may give better chances than others. The right course is to test as many possibilities as possible before committing yourself.

♠ A 3
♡ K 8 4
◊ 9 8 6 5 3
♣ Q J 5

```
      N
  W       E
      S
```

♠ K 6
♡ A Q 7 3
◊ A J 10 7
♣ K 7 2

Both Vulnerable
Dealer South

SOUTH	WEST	NORTH	EAST
1 NT	Pass	3 NT	Pass
Pass	Pass		

The opening lead of the queen of spades attacked the declarer's weak spot. Seeing little hope of nine tricks without making something of the diamonds, South won the first trick with the ace of spades and played a diamond for a finesse of the ten. West won with the queen and returned a spade. Now the party was nearly over. South crossed to the king of hearts and played another diamond, but when East showed out South found himself unable to make more than seven tricks.

The complete deal:

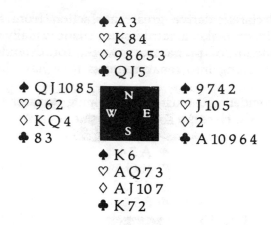

```
                    ♠ A 3
                    ♡ K 8 4
                    ◊ 9 8 6 5 3
                    ♣ Q J 5
    ♠ Q J 10 8 5                      ♠ 9 7 4 2
    ♡ 9 6 2          N               ♡ J 10 5
    ◊ K Q 4       W     E            ◊ 2
    ♣ 8 3            S               ♣ A 10 9 6 4
                    ♠ K 6
                    ♡ A Q 7 3
                    ◊ A J 10 7
                    ♣ K 7 2
```

No doubt it was unlucky to find both diamond honors badly placed, but South need not have committed himself so early to this particular line of play. The correct way to tackle the hand is to win the first trick with the king of spades and test the hearts by playing the ace, queen, and king. If the suit fails to break South can always fall back upon the double finesse in diamonds.

When in practice the hearts prove to break 3-3 South has no need to bother with the diamonds. He can make nine tricks in comfort by knocking out the ace of clubs.

MAXIM.	Keep your options open while testing the lie of the cards.

54. PRESERVING AN EXIT

Most declarers derive great satisfaction from throwing a defender in to make a fatal return. This usually involves a certain amount of preparatory work, for defenders do not oblige by leading into tenaces unless they have been left no alternative.

As a defender you must avoid helping declarer to eliminate your exit cards. Here is a common position.

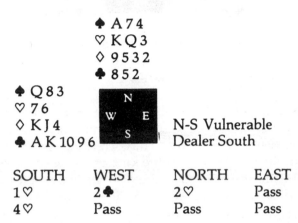

```
                ♠ A 7 4
                ♡ K Q 3
                ◊ 9 5 3 2
                ♣ 8 5 2
   ♠ Q 8 3
   ♡ 7 6
   ◊ K J 4          N-S Vulnerable
   ♣ A K 10 9 6     Dealer South
```

SOUTH	WEST	NORTH	EAST
1♡	2♣	2♡	Pass
4♡	Pass	Pass	Pass

West starts with the ace of clubs on which East plays the three and South the four. How should he continue?

From the play to the first trick it appears that East has three clubs and South two. It might therefore seem safe to continue with the king and another club rather than break a new suit.

It is safe in the sense that it gives South no immediate advantage, but in the long term it could help him to eliminate West's exit cards. The diamond holding is vulnerable, and West should see that he may be subject to a throw-in unless he defends as passively as possible.

The most passive defense is to switch to a trump. This can cost nothing. The declarer has no way of disposing of his second club loser, and the trump switch may be vital for the defense.

The complete deal:

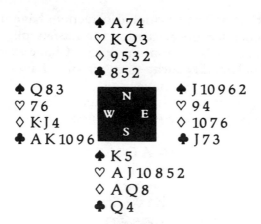

```
                    ♠ A 7 4
                    ♡ K Q 3
                    ◊ 9 5 3 2
                    ♣ 8 5 2
   ♠ Q 8 3          N          ♠ J 10 9 6 2
   ♡ 7 6        W       E       ♡ 9 4
   ◊ K·J 4                      ◊ 10 7 6
   ♣ A K 10 9 6      S          ♣ J 7 3
                    ♠ K 5
                    ♡ A J 10 8 5 2
                    ◊ A Q 8
                    ♣ Q 4
```

You see what happens if West continues with the king and another club? Declarer ruffs, plays three rounds of spades, ruffing in hand, and draws trumps ending in dummy. Then he plays a small diamond, inserting the eight if East plays low and covering with the queen if East plays the ten. Either way, West is thrown in to make a fatal return, and all because he helped declarer to eliminate his exit cards.

The difference on a trump return is that declarer is unable to eliminate both black suits and retain a trump in dummy. No matter how he plays the defenders must take four tricks.

MAXIM.	Don't help declarer to eliminate your exit cards.

55. NOT SO SAFE

One might expect international players to have no difficulty in recognizing the proper occasion for a safety play, but this is not always the case. In a European Championship match between Poland and Norway there was no swing on this hand, although there might well have been.

♠ 9 7 6
♡ 6 2
◇ A Q 10 7 3
♣ A 10 7

```
      N
   W     E
      S
```

♠ A K 8
♡ K 4 3
◇ J 5 4 2
♣ Q J 6

E-W Vulnerable
Dealer North

WEST	NORTH	EAST	SOUTH
	Pass	2♡ *	2NT
Pass	3 NT	Pass	Pass
Pass			

* weak two bid

In the other room the Poles had bid to five diamonds which proved to be a trick too high. The Norwegians therefore had the chance of a big gain if they could make their contract of three notrump.

West led the queen of hearts and East overtook with the ace in order to continue the suit, driving out the king on the third round. The declared played a small diamond to dummy's ten, and the writing was on the wall when East showed out. Having no more than four diamonds to cash, South had to fall back upon the club finesse, but his luck had run out. East produced the king of clubs and cashed enough hearts to put the contract two down.

The complete deal:

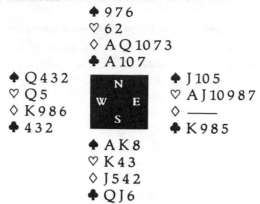

```
                 ♠ 9 7 6
                 ♡ 6 2
                 ◊ A Q 10 7 3
                 ♣ A 10 7
   ♠ Q 4 3 2         N          ♠ J 10 5
   ♡ Q 5          W     E       ♡ A J 10 9 8 7
   ◊ K 9 8 6         S          ◊ ——
   ♣ 4 3 2                      ♣ K 9 8 5
                 ♠ A K 8
                 ♡ K 4 3
                 ◊ J 5 4 2
                 ♣ Q J 6
```

The neglect of a routine safety play was responsible for the loss of the contract. South can guard against the possibility of four diamonds with West by leading the jack of diamonds on the first round. West has to cover with the king, and when East shows out the bad break is revealed. Now South can use his spade entries to finesse twice more against the nine and eight of diamonds, thus making five tricks in the suit.

MAXIM.　**Learn by heart the safety plays that cater for bad breaks.**

---

56. PROBLEM DEFERRED

Some players are strangely reluctant to use a forcing takeout. The declarer claimed he was unlucky on the following hand, but his partner had another word for it.

```
                        ♠ ——
                        ♡ A 8 6 3
                        ◇ A Q J 8 7 4
                        ♣ 10 9 4
        ♠ A 9 8 3                    ♠ 7 4 2
        ♡ 10 9 2          N          ♡ K Q J 7
        ◇ 10 9 5      W       E      ◇ 6 2
        ♣ K 8 3           S          ♣ Q J 7 5
                        ♠ K Q J 10 6 5
                        ♡ 5 4
N-S Vulnerable          ◇ K 3
Dealer North            ♣ A 6 2
```

WEST	NORTH	EAST	SOUTH
	1◇	1♡	1♠
2♡	3◇	Pass	4♠
Pass	Pass	Pass	

West led the ten of hearts, and South dared not duck for fear of a club switch. He won the first trick, came to hand with the king of diamonds and played the queen of spades. When this held the trick he continued with the jack of spades, hoping to slip past the ace once more. West had noticed his partner's six of diamonds on the first round of the suit, however, and he went up with the ace of spades in order to play a second diamond. This cut the last link with dummy and there was no way for South to avoid defeat.

South ran into a hot defense, it is true, but he should not have been in four spades in the first place. Five diamonds is a better contract with eleven tricks available even on a club lead. Three notrump can also be made as the cards lie.

The enemy interference did not help, but South's problem stemmed mainly from the fact that he left himself with no good way of expressing his values on the second round. Hence his unilateral decision to play in four spades.

As is often the case, the bidding would have been much simpler if South had forced by jumping to two spades on the first round. This is invariably the right course when a player has game values and a single-suited hand with or without support for his partner's suit. The force saves space in the long run. Whether West contests with three hearts or not, South has time both to rebid his spades and, eventually, to support his partner's diamonds.

MAXIM. Force immediately when you have game values and a single-suited hand.

---

57. MAY THE FORCE BE WITH YOU

Many an impossible contract is allowed to slip home because a defender does not carry his thought-processes quite far enough. Here is an example.

```
                    ♠ Q 10 3
                    ♡ 8 4
                    ◇ A K J 10 7 5 4
                    ♣ 6
                                      ♠ 7 6
                             N        ♡ A K 6 3
                         W       E    ◇ Q 9 2
Neither Vulnerable           S        ♣ A 7 4 2
Dealer South
```

SOUTH	WEST	NORTH	EAST
1♣	Pass	1◇	Pass
1♠	Pass	3◇	Pass
3♠	Pass	4♠	Pass
Pass	Pass		

West led the jack of hearts and East took the first two tricks, South playing the queen on the second round. Aware of the menace of the long diamond suit, East decided that the best chance for the defense was to force dummy to ruff. Accordingly he cashed the ace of clubs and then played a third heart.

This defense was not good enough, for predictably South had a 5-2-1-5 distribution with all the missing trump honors. He was able to ruff the third heart high, cash two high trumps and then play on diamonds, ruffing the third round high and returning to dummy with the queen of spades to enjoy the established diamonds.

The complete deal:

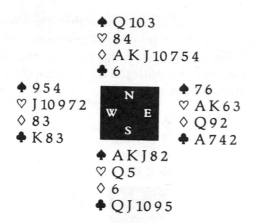

```
                ♠ Q 10 3
                ♡ 8 4
                ◊ A K J 10 7 5 4
                ♣ 6
  ♠ 9 5 4          N          ♠ 7 6
  ♡ J 10 9 7 2   W   E        ♡ A K 6 3
  ◊ 8 3              S         ◊ Q 9 2
  ♣ K 8 3                      ♣ A 7 4 2
                ♠ A K J 8 2
                ♡ Q 5
                ◊ 6
                ♣ Q J 10 9 5
```

The idea of forcing dummy to ruff was a good one, but East attacked in the wrong suit. Dummy can be forced only in clubs, and East has to underlead his ace of clubs at trick three to bring effective pressure to bear. West wins with the king and returns the suit, and there is no way for South to make more than nine tricks.

This defense may succeed even if West has the queen of clubs instead of the king.

MAXIM.   **Assume partner has the right cards when you need to play a forcing defense.**

---

58. TELESCOPING LOSERS

Prospects may appear bleak when there is a sure loser in trumps as well as a loser in one of the side suits, but it is sometimes possible to compress the two losers into one. The idea is to give the defender with the trump trick the opportunity to ruff losers rather than winners.

♠ 7 6 5
♡ 8 6 4 3
◊ K 5 2
♣ K 9 7

```
      N
  W       E
      S
```

♠ A K Q 4 2
♡ A

Both Vulnerable ◊ A Q 6 3
Dealer South ♣ A Q 3

SOUTH	WEST	NORTH	EAST
2♣	Pass	2◊	Pass
2♠	Pass	2 NT	Pass
3◊	Pass	3♠	Pass
4♣	Pass	4◊	Pass
4♡	Pass	5♣	Pass
6♠	Pass	Pass	Pass

West leads the queen of hearts to declarer's ace. Both defenders follow to the ace of spades, but West discards a club on the second round. How sould South continue?

Realizing that he could not afford a diamond loser, declarer tested the suit by cashing the ace and playing a second diamond to the king. But East ruffed this trick and returned his last trump, and there was no way for South to avoid the loss of a further trick.

The full hand:

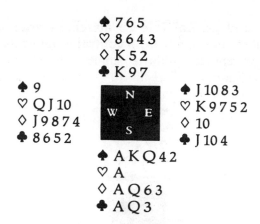

♠ 7 6 5
♡ 8 6 4 3
◊ K 5 2
♣ K 9 7

♠ 9
♡ Q J 10
◊ J 9 8 7 4
♣ 8 6 5 2

♠ J 10 8 3
♡ K 9 7 5 2
◊ 10
♣ J 10 4

♠ A K Q 4 2
♡ A
◊ A Q 6 3
♣ A Q 3

This was a case of faulty timing. South catered for the possibility of East having a doubleton diamond, failing to see that the club entry in dummy enabled him to cope with a 5-1 diamond break. He should have started the suit with a small diamond to the king and played the second round from dummy. The difference is that if East ruffs he will be ruffing a loser and there will be no further trick for the defense.

East will probably discard a club instead of ruffing, in which case South can win, return to dummy with the king of clubs and repeat the maneuver by leading the remaining diamond. If East discards again, South wins and ruffs his losing diamond with dummy's last trump. East may over-ruff but that is the only trick for the defense.

MAXIM.   **Make the defenders ruff losers, not winners.**

---

59. MAKING AN EXCEPTION

It is a sound general rule to attack in your longest and strongest suit against a notrump contract, but every rule has its exceptions. A defender paid the penalty for lack of flexibility on the following hand.

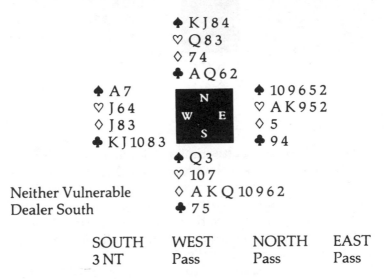

```
              ♠ K J 8 4
              ♡ Q 8 3
              ◊ 7 4
              ♣ A Q 6 2
  ♠ A 7                      ♠ 10 9 6 5 2
  ♡ J 6 4        N           ♡ A K 9 5 2
  ◊ J 8 3      W   E         ◊ 5
  ♣ K J 10 8 3   S           ♣ 9 4
              ♠ Q 3
              ♡ 10 7
Neither Vulnerable   ◊ A K Q 10 9 6 2
Dealer South  ♣ 7 5
```

SOUTH	WEST	NORTH	EAST
3 NT	Pass	Pass	Pass

South opened with a 'gambling' three notrump, showing a solid minor suit with little outside strength. Holding stoppers or at least semi-stoppers in all three side suits, North decided to stick it out.

West chose the orthodox lead of the jack of clubs but regretted it as soon as dummy went down. The declarer took his only chance by finessing the queen of clubs and when this stood up he had his nine tricks.

With all four hands on view it is clear that a heart lead would have been a happier choice for the defense. After a heart to the king and a spade back to the ace, the play of the jack of hearts enables the defenders to take the first six tricks.

It is not seriously suggested that West should lead a heart rather than a club, for he has no way of divining that this would work out well. What a defender should try to do in such a situation is to avoid committing himself to one particular line of defense. West keeps all his options open as far as possible if he starts with the ace of spades.

The sight of dummy should now help him to find the right continuation. On the actual hand it is clear that the only hope for the defense lies in the heart suit. A switch to the jack of hearts puts the contract two down.

With a different dummy it might have been a spade continuation or a club shift that was indicated.

Against a gambling three notrump bid, or indeed a high preemptive bid of any kind, it usually pays to lead an ace in an effort to retain the lead and have a look at dummy.

MAXIM. When opponents pre-empt, lead an ace if you have one.

---

60. THAT EXTRA TRICK

Good bidding at the slam level is the exception rather than the rule, particularly where a choice of suits is involved. Through lack of imagination players often fail to form a really accurate estimate of the number of tricks that will be available in each denomination. See what happened on this hand from a team-of-four match.

```
                    ♠ J 10 5
                    ♡ A J 10 4 2
                    ◊ A 8 7
                    ♣ 7 4
        ♠ 8 6              N          ♠ 7 3 2
        ♡ 9 8 6 3                     ♡ 5
        ◊ K 9 4 3      W       E      ◊ Q J 10 6 5
        ♣ Q J 6              S        ♣ K 10 5 2
                    ♠ A K Q 9 4
                    ♡ K Q 7
Both Vulnerable     ◊ 2
Dealer South        ♣ A 9 8 3
```

Room 1	SOUTH	WEST	NORTH	EAST
	1♠	Pass	2♡	Pass
	3♣	Pass	3♠	Pass
	4 NT	Pass	5♡	Pass
	5 NT	Pass	6♣	Pass
	6♠	Pass	Pass	Pass

When his partner showed two aces in response to the Blackwood four notrump enquiry, South could count twelve tricks with some assurance — five spades, five hearts and the minor suit aces. With visions of a grand slam he tried again with a bid of five notrump but settled at the six-level when North denied a king.

There was nothing to the play. South won the club lead, drew trumps, discarded two clubs on the long hearts and conceded a club at the end.

South was happy enough with his score of 1430 until he compared scores at the end and discovered that his team had

lost 13 IMP's on the board. In the other room the bidding had
gone as follows:

Room 2	SOUTH	WEST	NORTH	EAST
	1♠	Pass	2♡	Pass
	3♣	Pass	3♠	Pass
	4 NT	Pass	5♡	Pass
	5 NT	Pass	6♣	Pass
	7♡	Pass	Pass	Pass

The first four rounds of bidding were the same, but in this
room South realized that an extra trick would be made in hearts
by virtue of a diamond ruff in the short trump hand. Since he
had no objection to his partner playing an occasional hand,
South bid seven hearts and was rewarded with a score of 2210.

MAXIM. Other things being equal, choose the trump suit
that will enable you to ruff in the short trump
hand.

---

61. A TENSE GAME

Playing at a low level does not always make for a quiet game. A redoubled contract provided the setting for some interesting play and defense on this hand from a tough pairs tournament.

```
                    ♠ A 8 6
                    ♡ J 9 2
                    ◇ 7 3 2
                    ♣ K 8 7 3
    ♠ J 5 4 2          N          ♠ 9 7 3
    ♡ Q 10 6 3      W     E       ♡ K 5
    ◇ A J 6            S          ◇ Q 10 9 4
    ♣ A 5                         ♣ Q 10 9 2
                    ♠ K Q 10
                    ♡ A 8 7 4
Both Vulnerable     ◇ K 8 5
Dealer North        ♣ J 6 4
```

WEST	NORTH	EAST	SOUTH
	Pass	Pass	1 NT*
Pass	Pass	Dbl	Redbl
Pass	Pass	Pass	

*12-14 HCP

East's double was mandatory under his methods, for he and his partner had agreed never to defend against one notrump undoubled. North and South, naturally, had vowed never to play in one notrump doubled. South's redouble was obligatory under the partnership methods, the option to remove it lying with North. Such arrangements certainly make for a tense game.

West led the three of hearts to the nine, king, and ace. South immediately played a club to dummy's king. When this won, a second club went to West, who exited with the queen and another heart. The declarer played off three rounds of spades ending in hand, and then put West in with the fourth heart. After cashing his long spade, West had to open up the diamonds and concede a seventh trick to declarer.

The declarer played well in removing West's club exit at an

early stage. Nevertheless, West had the opportunity to gain 400 on the hand instead of losing 710. When in with the ace of clubs, he had only to lead the six or the jack of diamonds in order to gather seven tricks for the defense.

The jack is the better card, for it is then easy for East to put on the queen (if West leads the six, East has to find the double-dummy play of the nine). If South wins, he can cash only six tricks before conceding the remainder to the defense. If South holds up on the first round of diamonds, East can cash two further tricks in clubs before reverting to diamonds, again making sure of seven tricks for the defense.

MAXIM.	When a throw-in is inevitable, try and derive some advantage from it.

62. THE BIDDING TELLS A STORY

When a declarer has to choose between alternative lines of play he will often find it helpful to reflect on the bidding. Sometimes it is a failure to bid that supplies the vital clue to the location of the missing high cards.

```
              ♠ K 3
              ♡ 10 8 6 5
              ◇ K Q 7 2
              ♣ J 4 3

              ┌─────────┐
              │    N    │
              │ W     E │
              │    S    │
              └─────────┘

              ♠ A J 9
              ♡ A Q J 9 4 3
              ◇ 8 3
              ♣ 8 2
```

Neither Vulnerable
Dealer West

WEST	NORTH	EAST	SOUTH
1♣	Pass	Pass	2♡
Pass	3♡	Pass	4♡
Pass	Pass	Pass	

West attacked with top clubs, South ruffing the third round as East followed suit. How should South continue?

At the table South crossed to the king of spades and ran the ten of hearts, losing to the king. There was no way of avoiding a diamond loser and the contract went quietly one down.

Unlucky? Not really. In his eagerness to deploy the percentage play in trumps South missed the best chance of making his contract. On this type of hand the trump decision should be delayed until the missing ace has been located.

The complete deal:

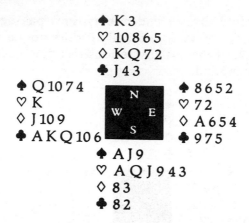

```
                    ♠ K 3
                    ♡ 10 8 6 5
                    ◊ K Q 7 2
                    ♣ J 4 3
   ♠ Q 10 7 4                       ♠ 8 6 5 2
   ♡ K                              ♡ 7 2
   ◊ J 10 9                         ◊ A 6 5 4
   ♣ A K Q 10 6                     ♣ 9 7 5
                    ♠ A J 9
                    ♡ A Q J 9 4 3
                    ◊ 8 3
                    ♣ 8 2
```

The correct play at trick two is a diamond, not a spade. If West produces the ace, South will eventually take the trump finesse. When East, against all expectations, produces the ace of diamonds South knows at once how to handle the trumps. Holding an ace and a king East would never have passed his partner's opening bid. The king of hearts is therefore marked in the West hand, and South's only remaining chance is that it will drop under the ace.

MAXIM. Remember the bidding when trying to locate key cards.

---

63. BIRD IN HAND

The prime duty of a defender, even in a pairs game, is to defeat the enemy contract. Normally it does not pay to try for extra undertricks if there is any serious risk involved. See what happened on this hand.

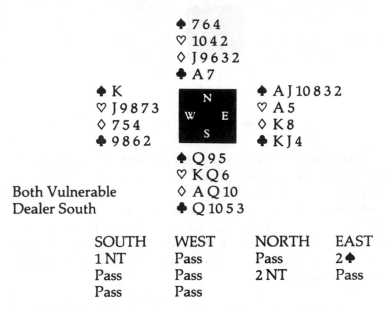

```
                        ♠ 7 6 4
                        ♡ 10 4 2
                        ◇ J 9 6 3 2
                        ♣ A 7
        ♠ K                             ♠ A J 10 8 3 2
        ♡ J 9 8 7 3      N              ♡ A 5
        ◇ 7 5 4        W   E            ◇ K 8
        ♣ 9 8 6 2        S              ♣ K J 4
                        ♠ Q 9 5
                        ♡ K Q 6
Both Vulnerable         ◇ A Q 10
Dealer South            ♣ Q 10 5 3
```

SOUTH	WEST	NORTH	EAST
1 NT	Pass	Pass	2 ♠
Pass	Pass	2 NT	Pass
Pass	Pass		

This is a fairly typical pairs auction. South's opening bid of one notrump was passed round to East, who sensibly chose to compete with two spades. North felt that his side might have the balance of power and contested further with two notrump.

Against this optimistic contract West led the king of spades, causing East to wish he had doubled. Anxious to direct a club switch, East played the two of spades on the first trick, relying on his partner to pick up the suit-preference indications. The club switch duly came, and when East was allowed to score the club king he switched promptly back to the ace and another spade.

Winning the queen of spades, South entered dummy with the ace of clubs, finessed the queen of diamonds and cashed the diamond ace, felling the king. He was then able to cash two more clubs and three more diamonds to make his contract with an overtrick, causing East to feel thankful that he had not doubled after all.

This was a poor effort by East. He can count six sure tricks for the defense if he overtakes his partner's king of spades and continues with the jack, and that is the only sensible course of action.

| MAXIM. | The top defensive priority is to defeat the contract. |

64. DEED OF TRANSFER

On the following hand the declarer was convinced that he had a choice between two risky courses of action. He failed to see that a third option — a completely safe one — was available to him.

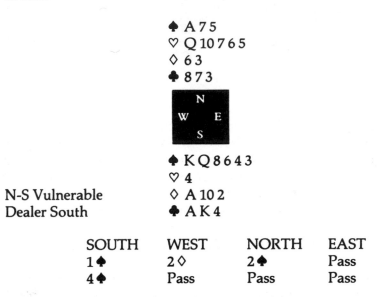

♠ A 7 5
♡ Q 10 7 6 5
♢ 6 3
♣ 8 7 3

♠ K Q 8 6 4 3
♡ 4
♢ A 10 2
♣ A K 4

N-S Vulnerable
Dealer South

SOUTH	WEST	NORTH	EAST
1♠	2♢	2♠	Pass
4♠	Pass	Pass	Pass

West led the king of diamonds which was allowed to hold the first trick. South took his ace on the second round and cashed the king of spades, on which West played the nine and East the two. Although there appeared to be little chance of setting up a heart trick, South played his heart at trick three in order to establish sound communications.

West won and persisted with a third round of diamonds, giving South a bit of a headache. Although East had not echoed in diamonds, South suspected that he might have started with a doubleton and would over-ruff dummy if given the chance. South therefore ruffed the third diamond with the ace of spades, hoping for a 2-2 break in trumps. Alas, his hopes were not realized for the complete deal was as follows:

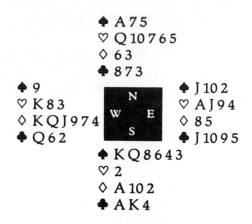

♠ A 7 5
♡ Q 10 7 6 5
◊ 6 3
♣ 8 7 3

♠ 9
♡ K 8 3
◊ K Q J 9 7 4
♣ Q 6 2

♠ J 10 2
♡ A J 9 4
◊ 8 5
♣ J 10 9 5

♠ K Q 8 6 4 3
♡ 2
◊ A 10 2
♣ A K 4

West was marked with long diamonds and East was likely to have three trumps, which made South's line of play a poor gamble. The right way to try for a tenth trick is by ruffing a club rather than a diamond. Just discard a club from dummy on the third diamond and the defenders are helpless. Whether West continues with a fourth diamond or switches to something else, declarer is always able to score a tenth trick by ruffing his losing club with dummy's small trump.

MAXIM.   **Transfer a ruff to a safe suit whenever possible.**

---

65. HELPING OUT

Many players apparently persist in regarding their partners as a third opponent. This perhaps explains why the correct defense was often missed on this hand from a recent tournament.

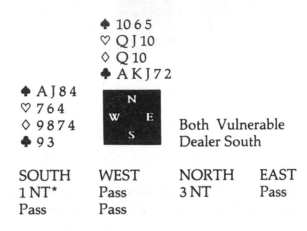

```
              ♠ 10 6 5
              ♡ Q J 10
              ◇ Q 10
              ♣ A K J 7 2
♠ A J 8 4      ┌──────────┐
♡ 7 6 4        │    N     │
◇ 9 8 7 4      │ W     E  │     Both Vulnerable
♣ 9 3          │    S     │     Dealer South
               └──────────┘
```

SOUTH	WEST	NORTH	EAST
1 NT*	Pass	3 NT	Pass
Pass	Pass		

*12-14 HCP

South opened with a weak notrump and North raised directly to game. The popular lead was the nine of diamonds, which was covered by the ten and jack and won by South with the king.

The four of clubs was played for a finesse of the jack. East won with the queen and returned the two of spades on which South played the three and West the jack. How should West continue?

In practice a number of West players went wrong by continuing with the ace and another spade. This blocked the spade suit and allowed declarer to make nine tricks with the aid of the heart finesse.

The complete deal:

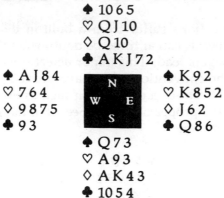

```
                    ♠ 10 6 5
                    ♡ Q J 10
                    ◇ Q 10
                    ♣ A K J 7 2
    ♠ A J 8 4           N           ♠ K 9 2
    ♡ 7 6 4         W       E       ♡ K 8 5 2
    ◇ 9 8 7 5           S           ◇ J 6 2
    ♣ 9 3                           ♣ Q 8 6
                    ♠ Q 7 3
                    ♡ A 9 3
                    ◇ A K 4 3
                    ♣ 10 5 4
```

The West players who misdefended presumably placed their partners with four spades headed by the queen. It did not occur to them that with the king and one other spade South would surely have taken his best chance by going up with the king.

However, the East players were guilty of creating an unnecessary problem for their partners. Having decided to go for the setting tricks in spades, they should have clarified the position by playing the spade king instead of the two. Now it is impossible for West to go astray.

MAXIM.   Choose the play that makes life easy for partner.

---

66. CONVENTIONAL WISDOM

Bidding conventions suffer from a built-in disadvantage in that the artificial bids can at times be doubled by the opponents to direct a damaging lead. This minor defect does not curb the popularity of the conventions that have proved themselves to be worth using. Even so, a convention such as Stayman should be reserved for the proper occasion. See what happened on this hand from a team game.

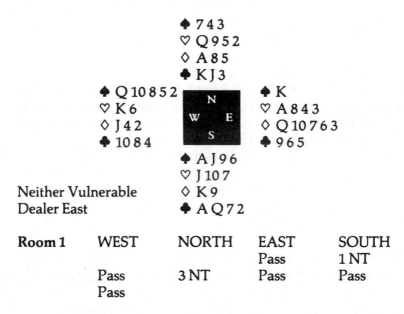

```
                         ♠ 7 4 3
                         ♡ Q 9 5 2
                         ◊ A 8 5
                         ♣ K J 3
        ♠ Q 10 8 5 2              ♠ K
        ♡ K 6                     ♡ A 8 4 3
        ◊ J 4 2                   ◊ Q 10 7 6 3
        ♣ 10 8 4                  ♣ 9 6 5
                         ♠ A J 9 6
                         ♡ J 10 7
Neither Vulnerable       ◊ K 9
Dealer East              ♣ A Q 7 2
```

Room 1	WEST	NORTH	EAST	SOUTH
			Pass	1 NT
	Pass	3 NT	Pass	Pass
	Pass			

West made the natural lead of the five of spades and South captured the king with his ace. He tackled the hearts, knocking out the ace and king to establish two tricks in the suit which, with two diamonds, four clubs and a spade made his total up to nine.

Room 2	WEST	NORTH	EAST	SOUTH
			Pass	1 NT
	Pass	2 ♣	Pass	2 ♠
	Pass	3 NT	Pass	Pass
	Pass			

In the other room North chose to flourish Stayman, which proved to be a costly mistake. It was not, in this case, that anyone was able to double. But West, warned against the spade lead by South's bid, decided to try one of the minors. The only thing to guide him was the fact that his partner had *not* doubled the Stayman two club bid for a lead. West therefore led the two of diamonds and this turned out to be a happy choice for his side. The defenders were able to set up three diamond tricks to add to their two top hearts, putting the contract one down.

It is a mistake to use Stayman on flat, 4-3-3-3 hands that have enough power for game. Stayman is unlikely to gain much even if a 4-4 fit is found, and there is always the real danger of giving away vital information to the enemy. Just go straight to three notrump on such hands.

MAXIM.   Avoid using Stayman on balanced game hands.

---

67. DISAPPEARING TRICKS

Holding a double stopper in trumps behind declarer a defender naturally expects to score a couple of trumps tricks, but it does not always work out like that. See what happened on this hand.

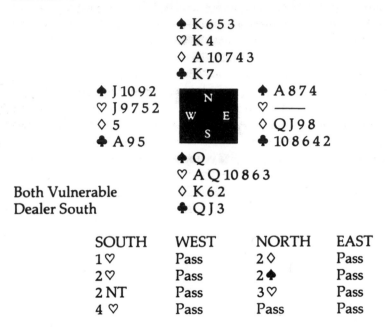

```
                    ♠ K 6 5 3
                    ♡ K 4
                    ◊ A 10 7 4 3
                    ♣ K 7
   ♠ J 10 9 2              N          ♠ A 8 7 4
   ♡ J 9 7 5 2      W           E     ♡ ———
   ◊ 5                     S          ◊ Q J 9 8
   ♣ A 9 5                            ♣ 10 8 6 4 2
                    ♠ Q
                    ♡ A Q 10 8 6 3
                    ◊ K 6 2
                    ♣ Q J 3
```

Both Vulnerable
Dealer South

SOUTH	WEST	NORTH	EAST
1 ♡	Pass	2 ◊	Pass
2 ♡	Pass	2 ♠	Pass
2 NT	Pass	3 ♡	Pass
4 ♡	Pass	Pass	Pass

West led the jack of spades to his partner's ace and East returned the suit, South discarding a diamond as dummy's king won. The play of the king of hearts revealed the bad trump break, and the declarer realized that he needed a trump end-play against West in order to make his contract.

South ruffed a spade at trick four and then played a club to dummy's king. When this held, a second club was played to the queen and ace. West switched to a diamond, but South won in dummy, ruffed another spade in hand and cashed the jack of clubs. At this stage West had nothing but trumps left, and when the king of diamonds was played he had to ruff and return a trump into South's tenace, yielding the rest of the tricks.

At the outset the defense appeared to have two trump tricks and two aces, but one of the trump tricks failed to materialize.

Was there anything West could have done about it?

West might have recognized that his trump holding was of the insecure type that often lends itself to a trump end-play. The remedy is simple. On this type of hand one should not lead long suits but go for ruffs from the start. If West begins with the singleton diamond, East can give him a diamond ruff when he gains the lead with the ace of spades. West will naturally take his ace of clubs next, and he cannot be denied a further trick in trumps.

MAXIM. Go for ruffs when you have a long but vulnerable trump holding.

---

68. CONTINGENCY PLAN

The declarer thought he had spotted the danger on the following hand, but his plan failed to cater to all possibilities.

♠ 10 4 3
♡ J 4
◇ J 10 7 6 2
♣ K 9 5

♠ A J 6
♡ K 9 8 3
◇ A Q 9 4
♣ A 10

N-S Vulnerable
Dealer East

WEST	NORTH	EAST	SOUTH
		1♠	Dbl
Pass	2◇	Pass	2 NT
Pass	3 NT	Pass	Pass
Pass			

South landed in a thin game when he considered his hand to be too strong for an immediate overcall of one notrump.

West led the eight of spades and South played low from dummy. He planned to hold off when East played the queen but to win the jack on the second round and tackle the diamonds. He would be safe even if the king of diamonds was off-side, for West would not have another spade to lead and South would eventually set up his ninth trick in hearts.

But something happened that South had not bargained for. East played the nine of spades at trick one, forcing South to win at once with the jack. Vaguely unhappy, South crossed to the king of clubs and ran the jack of diamonds. Sure enough, West had the king and was able to play a second spade to the queen and ace. South had only eight tricks, and East scored enough spades to defeat the game when he gained the lead with the heart ace.

The complete deal:

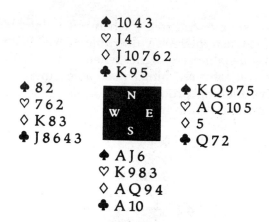

```
                    ♠ 10 4 3
                    ♡ J 4
                    ◊ J 10 7 6 2
                    ♣ K 9 5
    ♠ 8 2            N          ♠ K Q 9 7 5
    ♡ 7 6 2      W       E      ♡ A Q 10 5
    ◊ K 8 3          S          ◊ 5
    ♣ J 8 6 4 3                 ♣ Q 7 2
                    ♠ A J 6
                    ♡ K 9 8 3
                    ◊ A Q 9 4
                    ♣ A 10
```

East was right to maintain communications with his partner by playing low on the first round of spades. If South had foreseen this possibility he might have found the counter.

The correct play is the ten of spades from dummy at trick one. If East ducks, South can play a heart to his king, going at once for his ninth trick in hearts just in case there is a diamond loser. East cannot gain by playing the heart ace, and when South wins with the king he can switch to diamonds, playing the ace and queen from hand in case of a 4-0 break.

If West, against all expectations, turns up with the heart ace, South can be quite sure that the diamond finesse will work.

MAXIM. Look for a plan that can cope with any defense.

---

69. A TIME FOR BOLDNESS

Many players overcall freely when not vulnerable but draw in their horns when they are vulnerable, fearing a large penalty. It is true that penalties are higher when you are vulnerable, but so are the rewards for reaching a makeable game.

Aggressive bidding produced a double game swing on this hand from a team-of-four match.

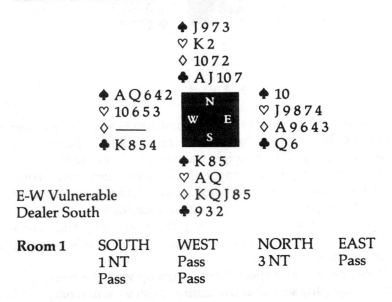

```
                      ♠ J 9 7 3
                      ♡ K 2
                      ◊ 10 7 2
                      ♣ A J 10 7
  ♠ A Q 6 4 2                        ♠ 10
  ♡ 10 6 5 3                         ♡ J 9 8 7 4
  ◊ ——                               ◊ A 9 6 4 3
  ♣ K 8 5 4                          ♣ Q 6
                      ♠ K 8 5
                      ♡ A Q
E-W Vulnerable        ◊ K Q J 8 5
Dealer South          ♣ 9 3 2
```

Room 1	SOUTH	WEST	NORTH	EAST
	1 NT	Pass	3 NT	Pass
	Pass	Pass		

West did not consider that he had the makings of a vulnerable overcall, and North raised his partner directly to three notrump. A heart lead would have defeated this contract, but West can hardly be blamed for leading a small spade to the ten and king. The declarer was then able to muster nine tricks by way of one spade, two hearts, four diamonds and two clubs.

Room 2	SOUTH	WEST	NORTH	EAST
	1 NT	2♣	Dbl	2◊
	Dbl	2♡	Pass	4♡
	Pass	Pass	Dbl	Pass
	Pass	Pass		

In this room West was made of sterner stuff. His conventional overcall of two clubs indicated a three-suited hand with shortage in one of the red suits. East temporized with a bid of two diamonds, but when his partner converted to hearts he raised all the way to game.

West won the diamond lead with the ace, discarding a club from his hand. He finessed the queen of spades, ruffed a spade and played a trump to South's queen. Ruffing the diamond return, West ruffed another spade and played a second round of trumps. When the outstanding honors fell together he had ten tricks.

MAXIM. Bid boldly when the rewards are greatest — when you are vulnerable.

70. KEEPING CONTROL

When the defenders are bound to score at least one trick in trumps, the timing of the concession of this trick may make a big difference to the outcome. See what happened to a careless declarer on this hand.

<pre>
                    ♠ A 7 2
                    ♡ K Q 5
                    ◇ 7 5 4
                    ♣ A 9 7 3
                    ┌───────────┐
                    │   N   │
                    │ W   E │
                    │   S   │
                    └───────────┘
                    ♠ Q 8 6 4 3
                    ♡ J 6 4
Both Vulnerable   ◇ A K Q 8
Dealer North   ♣ 6
</pre>

WEST	NORTH	EAST	SOUTH
	1♣	Pass	1♠
Pass	1 NT	Pass	3◇
Pass	3♠	Pass	4♠
Pass	Pass	Pass	

West led the ten of hearts to the queen and ace and East returned a heart to the jack. Believing that there would be no trouble if the spades were 3-2, declarer tried to cater for a singleton king in one hand or the other by cashing the ace on the first round. Both defenders followed with low spades, and a second spade was played to the queen and king. West unkindly cashed a third round of trumps, leaving South dependent on a 3-3 break in diamonds. Naturally there was no happy ending, for the complete deal was as follows:

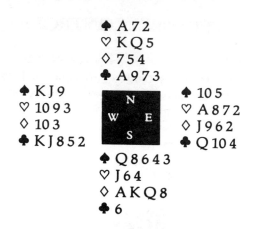

♠ A 7 2
♥ K Q 5
♦ 7 5 4
♣ A 9 7 3

♠ K J 9   ♠ 10 5
♥ 10 9 3   ♥ A 8 7 2
♦ 10 3   ♦ J 9 6 2
♣ K J 8 5 2   ♣ Q 10 4

♠ Q 8 6 4 3
♥ J 6 4
♦ A K Q 8
♣ 6

On this hand South should have been ready to trade the chance of finding West with a singleton king of spades for a better chance of success in the more probable 3-2 splits. If the spade honors lie badly, with the king over the queen, the spade ace is best taken on the second round rather than the first. This keeps control of the position and ensures that the fourth diamond can be ruffed in dummy if necessary.

South should have won the second heart in dummy and played a low spade from the table. The queen loses to West's king, but declarer wins the second round of trumps with the ace and plays on diamonds to make sure of ten tricks.

MAXIM.   Don't let the opponents draw a trump that may be needed for ruffing.

---

71. ATTACKING AN ENTRY

One of the most effective defensive techniques consists of forcing the declarer to use his entry cards before he is ready for them. A defender familiar with the technique would have done better on the following hand.

```
              ♠ 10 4
              ♡ Q 8 5 2
              ◊ K 8 2
              ♣ A Q 10 5
                            ♠ 8 7 5
                      N     ♡ A 10 9 3
                  W   E     ◊ A Q 7 3
                      S     ♣ 8 3
```

Both Vulnerable
Dealer North

WEST	NORTH	EAST	SOUTH
	Pass	Pass	1♠
Pass	2 NT	Pass	3♡
Pass	4♡	Pass	Pass
Pass			

West led the jack of diamonds to the king, ace and five. East continued with the queen of diamonds on which South played the six and West the four. What now?

In practice East continued with a third diamond, forcing declarer to ruff. This defense would have been successful if South had held only four hearts, but on the actual lie of the cards it was not good enough.

The complete deal:

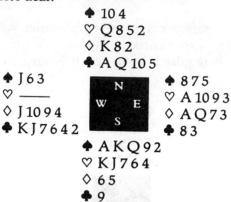

```
                    ♠ 10 4
                    ♡ Q 8 5 2
                    ◇ K 8 2
                    ♣ A Q 10 5
    ♠ J 6 3          N          ♠ 8 7 5
    ♡ —          W       E      ♡ A 10 9 3
    ◇ J 10 9 4       S          ◇ A Q 7 3
    ♣ K J 7 6 4 2               ♣ 8 3
                    ♠ A K Q 9 2
                    ♡ K J 7 6 4
                    ◇ 6 5
                    ♣ 9
```

Ruffing the third diamond, South played a low heart to the queen and ace. He won the spade return, crossed to the club ace and played the eight of hearts to the nine and jack. A third-round spade ruff gave South a further entry to dummy, and a finesse against the heart ten enabled him to claim his contract.

East should have seen the need to attack the entries in dummy in order to protect his trump holding. In the dangerous case where South has five hearts he can have no more than one club, and the correct move at trick three must be to lead a club into the jaws of dummy's tenace. Not being gifted with second sight, South can hardly take a deep finesse on the first round of trumps. If he plays the queen of hearts from the table, East can win and return a diamond or a spade. South can enter dummy only once more by means of a spade ruff, and East is assured of scoring a second trump trick.

MAXIM.   Attack the entries before declarer is ready to use them.

---

72. SAFETY FIRST

The common safety plays are well known and are seldom overlooked by experienced players. When a degree of improvisation is required, however, it is surprising how many players will come to grief.

```
              ♠ 8 7 3
              ♡ K J 9 2
              ◊ 7 5 4
              ♣ Q J 4
              ┌─────────┐
              │    N    │
              │ W     E │
              │    S    │
              └─────────┘
              ♠ A
              ♡ A 7 6 5 4
Both Vulnerable   ◊ K 6 2
Dealer South  ♣ A K 8 6
```

SOUTH	WEST	NORTH	EAST
1♡	Pass	2♡	Pass
4♡	Pass	Pass	Pass

West led the queen of spades. South thought he knew the right way to tackle the trumps here. A 2-2 break was quite probable and it could not be right to finesse into the East hand. If West had the queen guarded he was welcome to score a trick with it. So South cashed the ace of hearts at trick two and continued with a heart to the king.

After following with the heart ten, however, West showed out on the second round, marking East with a trump winner. South therefore had to fall back on the secondary chance that the clubs would divide evenly. But East ruffed the third club and switched to the jack of diamonds. Fearing the worst, South put up the king. Sure enough, the third chance failed when West produced the ace, and the defenders cashed three diamonds to put the contract one down.

The complete deal:

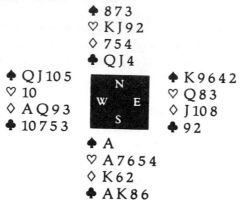

```
                    ♠ 873
                    ♡ KJ92
                    ◇ 754
                    ♣ QJ4
   ♠ QJ105                        ♠ K9642
   ♡ 10          N                ♡ Q83
   ◇ AQ93      W   E              ◇ J108
   ♣ 10753        S               ♣ 92
                    ♠ A
                    ♡ A7654
                    ◇ K62
                    ♣ AK86
```

Plenty of things had to go wrong for South to lose his game. Nevertheless, he failed to avail himself of an extra measure of safety. Once he has decided that he is not going to finesse into the East hand, there is no reason to start the trumps by cashing the ace. If South instead plays a low heart from hand at trick two, the appearance of the ten from West permits a perfect safety play. South wins in dummy with the king and returns the jack for a finesse against East.

As the cards lie this play brings in eleven tricks, and it would be good for ten tricks even if West had started with Q 10 doubleton and scored an unexpected trump trick.

MAXIM.   Where safety is concerned,
Let no stone be unturned.

151

73. UNDER THE CHOPPER

There are certain constantly-recurring situations in which a lapse of bidding judgement can be hideously expensive. See if you can spot the bid that did the damage on this hand from a team-of-four match.

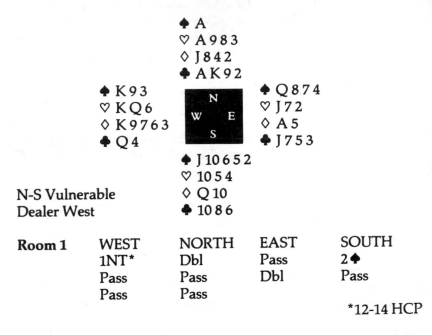

```
                    ♠ A
                    ♡ A 9 8 3
                    ◊ J 8 4 2
                    ♣ A K 9 2
    ♠ K 9 3                      ♠ Q 8 7 4
    ♡ K Q 6                      ♡ J 7 2
    ◊ K 9 7 6 3                  ◊ A 5
    ♣ Q 4                        ♣ J 7 5 3
                    ♠ J 10 6 5 2
                    ♡ 10 5 4
                    ◊ Q 10
                    ♣ 10 8 6
```

N-S Vulnerable
Dealer West

Room 1	WEST	NORTH	EAST	SOUTH
	1NT*	Dbl	Pass	2♠
	Pass	Pass	Dbl	Pass
	Pass	Pass		

*12-14 HCP

South did not have a happy time playing in two spades doubled. He was able to make no more than five tricks, thus conceding a penalty of 800 points.

Room 2	WEST	NORTH	EAST	SOUTH
	1 NT*	Dbl	Pass	Pass
	Pass			

*12-14 HCP

In the other room the bidding started in exactly the same way, but South passed his partner's double of one notrump. West made seven tricks for a score of 180 points, the total swing on the hand being 12 IMP's.

The pass is, of course, the only sensible action for South in the circumstances. It is a common mistake to take out into a five-card suit because of weakness. At this vulnerability South should pass all balanced and semi-balanced hands, taking out only if he has real distributional values.

It will never be a tragedy to allow declarer to play in one notrump doubled even if he can make an overtrick or two. But by bidding on this sort of hand a player lays his head on the chopping block.

MAXIM.   Pass partner's double of one notrump on all balanced and semi-balanced hands.

74. THE DEFENSE RESTS

It is natural and understandable for a defender to give priority to establishing his long suit again a notrump contract. What is natural is not always right, however, as a defender discovered on this hand from a match.

```
                          ♠ 6
                          ♡ J 7 3
                          ◇ Q 10 9 4
                          ♣ A K Q J 9
                                        ♠ K 9 4
                          N             ♡ A K 10 9 6 2
                      W       E         ◇ A K 3
Both Vulnerable           S             ♣ 5
Dealer East
```

WEST	NORTH	EAST	SOUTH
		1♡	1♠
Pass	2♣	2♡	2♠
Pass	3♡	Dbl	3 NT
Pass	Pass	Dbl	Pass
Pass	Pass		

West led the five of hearts in response to his partner's double and East won the first two tricks with the king and ace, South's queen falling on the second round. How should East continue?

In practice East continued with a third heart to clear the suit, expecting to inflict severe punishment on the impertinent game contract. But things did not work out quite as planned, for the complete deal was as follows:

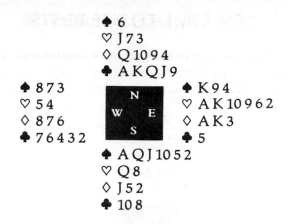

```
                    ♠ 6
                    ♡ J 7 3
                    ◇ Q 10 9 4
                    ♣ A K Q J 9
     ♠ 8 7 3          N          ♠ K 9 4
     ♡ 5 4       W         E      ♡ A K 10 9 6 2
     ◇ 8 7 6         S          ◇ A K 3
     ♣ 7 6 4 3 2                 ♣ 5
                    ♠ A Q J 10 5 2
                    ♡ Q 8
                    ◇ J 5 2
                    ♣ 10 8
```

When the declarer ran the clubs East was in trouble over his discards. Unable to spare a spade, he threw the losing diamond and the three established hearts. But this made the position quite obvious to the declarer. South finessed in spades and exited with a diamond, and after cashing his second diamond winner East had to concede two further tricks in spades.

If East had been on his toes he might have realized that he could not afford to knock out the heart stopper at trick three. The first priority was to cut the link between the two hands by playing a spade. After finessing in spades, South is poorly placed. He can continue with the spade ace and then run the clubs, settling for eight tricks, or he can play a diamond. In the latter case East can afford to knock out the heart stopper and the declarer makes no more than seven tricks.

MAXIM. Establish your long suit at notrump only if there is no more urgent job to be done.

---

75. A TIME TO IMPROVISE

The opening lead against a game contract can be a vital matter, and it is a subject that is sadly neglected in most of the text-books. Would you have done better than West on the following hand?

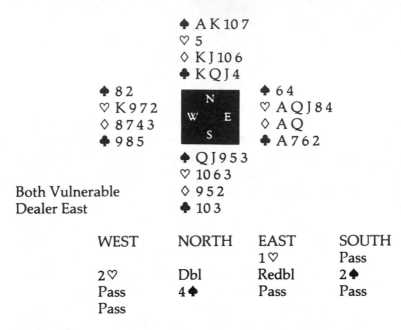

```
                     ♠ A K 10 7
                     ♡ 5
                     ◇ K J 10 6
                     ♣ K Q J 4
        ♠ 8 2                        ♠ 6 4
        ♡ K 9 7 2         N          ♡ A Q J 8 4
        ◇ 8 7 4 3     W       E      ◇ A Q
        ♣ 9 8 5           S          ♣ A 7 6 2
                     ♠ Q J 9 5 3
                     ♡ 10 6 3
Both Vulnerable      ◇ 9 5 2
Dealer East          ♣ 10 3
```

WEST	NORTH	EAST	SOUTH
		1♡	Pass
2♡	Dbl	Redbl	2♠
Pass	4♠	Pass	Pass
Pass			

West led the two of hearts to his partner's ace and East returned a trump. Declarer drew a second round of trumps and then turned his attention to the clubs, forcing out the ace. East was unable to attack the diamonds with any profit from his side of the table, and declarer eventually discarded two of his losing diamonds on the clubs. He thus made his contract, losing only one trick in each of the side suits.

There was nothing the defenders could do after the initial lead of a small heart. Clearly a diamond lead would have given the defenders four tricks, but how could West know that it was a diamond rather than a club lead that was required?

West could not know, of course, but he might have made an effort to find out. He knew from the bidding that most of the high cards would be on his left and that his partner might well need a lead through one of the side suits. It is the sort of situation in which one wants to lead an ace in order to retain the lead and have a look at dummy.

West does not have an ace, but he might have realized that the king of hearts could serve as well. The unorthodox lead of the king of hearts allows West to hold the lead, and the sight of dummy makes it clear that a diamond switch is required. Small points like this account for large swings.

MAXIM.   Be unorthodox when you need to retain the lead.

---

76. MENACING TRUMPS

When the defenders threaten a trump promotion it may be necessary to take evasive action. Few declarers took the right precautions on this hand from a tournament.

```
              ♠ Q 7 4
              ♥ Q 6 2
              ◊ Q J 8 3
              ♣ 7 5 4
```

```
                  N
              W       E
                  S
```

```
              ♠ 8 6
              ♥ K J 7 5 3
              ◊ A K 6 4
              ♣ A K
```

N-S Vulnerable
Dealer East

WEST	NORTH	EAST	SOUTH
		1♠	Dbl
Pass	1 NT	Pass	3♥
Pass	4♥	Pass	Pass
Pass			

The defenders attacked in spades and South ruffed low on the third round, breathing a sigh of relief when West followed suit. One declarer gave himself no chance when he played a low heart to the queen at trick four. East won the heart ace and a fourth spade promoted a second trump trick for the defense.

Another declarer did a little better by playing the king of hearts from hand at trick four. He would have been all right if East had held the ace of hearts doubleton. East had three hearts and West two, however, and a further spade lead enabled West to uppercut with his remaining trump to establish the setting trick.

The complete deal:

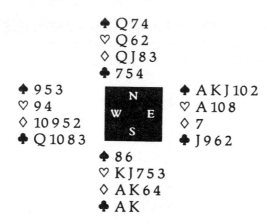

```
                    ♠ Q 7 4
                    ♡ Q 6 2
                    ◊ Q J 8 3
                    ♣ 7 5 4
    ♠ 9 5 3           N           ♠ A K J 10 2
    ♡ 9 4        W         E      ♡ A 10 8
    ◊ 10 9 5 2                    ◊ 7
    ♣ Q 10 8 3        S          ♣ J 9 6 2
                    ♠ 8 6
                    ♡ K J 7 5 3
                    ◊ A K 6 4
                    ♣ A K
```

With the ace of hearts marked in the East hand, South needs to play trumps through East if he is to avoid the trump promotion. The right move is a diamond to the jack at trick four and a small heart back. If East goes up with the ace and returns a spade, South can afford to ruff high and draw trumps.

Suppose East plays low on the first trump and the king wins. Should South continue with a low trump to the queen and ace? This works on the above layout since West is out of trumps, but if West had a third trump the defenders would still get their trump promotion. That's no good. Nor can it be right to play another diamond to the queen, hoping to repeat the trump play through East. This meets its just desserts when 'East ruffs the second diamond.

All South need do, in fact, is play the jack of trumps from hand on the second round. This restricts the defenders to one trump trick whether East's ace is doubleton or trebleton.

MAXIM. Try to slip past the enemy trump honors on the first round in order to avoid a promotion.

---

77. TRICKS FOR THE TAKING.

There may be more than one way of making the required number of tricks in a suit contract. Sometimes it is a matter of drawing trumps, sometimes of establishing a side suit, and sometimes a different approach is needed.

```
                    ♠ 7 5
                    ♡ 10 8 6 5 3
                    ◇ K 9 5
                    ♣ K 8 4
                        N
                    W       E
                        S
                    ♠ A K J 10 3
                    ♡ —
Both Vulnerable     ◇ A 10 7 6 2
Dealer South        ♣ A Q 6
```

SOUTH	WEST	NORTH	EAST
1♠	Pass	1 NT	Pass
3◇	Pass	3♠	Pass
4♠	Pass	Pass	Pass

West led the queen of hearts for declarer to ruff. South knew better than to consider finessing in trumps at the risk of losing control. He had been taught to set up the side suit early on two-suited hands, so he played the ace, king and another diamond. East won the third round, West discarding a club, and another heart forced declared to ruff again. Too late, South awoke to the fact that he was destined to lose trump control anyway. As a last desperate fling he crossed to the king of clubs and played a trump to the jack, hoping to find the queen on side and a 3-3 break. No luck! The contract had to go two down, for the complete hand was as follows:

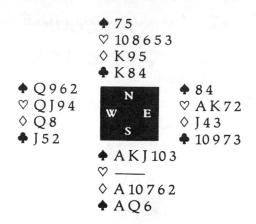

```
              ♠ 7 5
              ♡ 10 8 6 5 3
              ◇ K 9 5
              ♣ K 8 4
♠ Q 9 6 2        N        ♠ 8 4
♡ Q J 9 4    W       E    ♡ A K 7 2
◇ Q 8            S        ◇ J 4 3
♣ J 5 2                   ♣ 10 9 7 3
              ♠ A K J 10 3
              ♡ —
              ◇ A 10 7 6 2
              ♣ A Q 6
```

On any other attack South would have been right to establish the side suit. There is little point in this, however, once hearts have been led. The force at trick one puts the defenders a tempo ahead, and South cannot reasonably expect to draw trumps.

The alternative — and a very good alternative — is to accept the force and help it along, aiming to make five trumps tricks along with five outside winners. After ruffing the first heart, South can cash the ace and king of diamonds, ruff a heart with the ten of spades, play three rounds of clubs ending in dummy, and ruff another club with the jack of spades. That adds up to eight tricks, and the ace and king of spades are still to come.

MAXIM.   When a force is inevitable, relax and enjoy it.

161

78. COUNTER-COUP

Careful defense is the only good answer to optimistic bidding. Take the West seat on this hand and see how you would have fared.

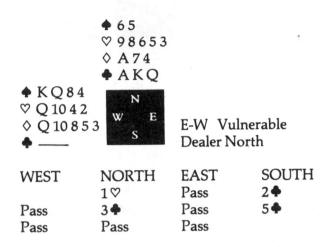

```
                    ♠ 6 5
                    ♡ 9 8 6 5 3
                    ◇ A 7 4
                    ♣ A K Q
    ♠ K Q 8 4       ┌──────────┐
    ♡ Q 10 4 2      │    N     │
    ◇ Q 10 8 5 3    │ W     E  │      E-W  Vulnerable
    ♣ ———           │    S     │      Dealer North
                    └──────────┘
```

WEST	NORTH	EAST	SOUTH
	1♡	Pass	2♣
Pass	3♣	Pass	5♣
Pass	Pass	Pass	

West led the five of diamonds to dummy's ace, East following with the nine and South with the jack. Declarer played a low heart, East winning with the ace while South played the jack, and East returned the three of clubs to dummy's queen. South ruffed a diamond in hand, cashed the ace of spades and continued with the jack of spades, East following low-high. In with the queen of spades, how should West continue?

On the bidding and play it seemed clear that declarer had started with six clubs and four spades. He had scored two aces in the side-suits and had the king of hearts to come. If his trumps were solid enough, there could be no way of preventing him from making the rest of his trumps on a cross-ruff. East could have a potential trump trick, of course, in which it will be vital not to help declarer shorten his trumps by returning a red card. There is an indication in that declarer has already taken a diamond ruff.

Seeing the danger, West found the only defense to beat the contract when he returned the king of spades.

The complete hand:

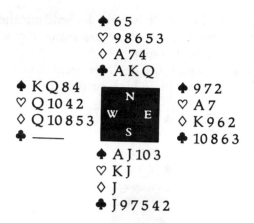

♠ 6 5
♡ 9 8 6 5 3
◇ A 7 4
♣ A K Q

♠ K Q 8 4   ♠ 9 7 2
♡ Q 10 4 2   ♡ A 7
◇ Q 10 8 5 3   ◇ K 9 6 2
♣ ——   ♣ 10 8 6 3

♠ A J 10 3
♡ K J
◇ J
♣ J 9 7 5 4 2

The return of a heart or a diamond would have enabled declarer to make his contract on a cross-ruff, picking up East's trumps by a coup at the end. The return of a low spade would also have let the contract home, for South would have won in hand with the ten, cashed the heart king, played a club to the king, ruffed a red card, ruffed his last spade in dummy with the ace of clubs, and led through East at trick twelve to pick up the last two tricks.

West's play of the king of spades set up South's ten as a winner, but it did declarer no good at all. The timing of the trump coup was upset and South eventually had to concede a trick to East's ten of trumps.

MAXIM.   Don't help to shorten declarer's trumps when partner may have a vulnerable trump stopper.

---

79. VAIN HOLD-UP

Declarers are taught that it is right to hold up the ace in an enemy suit. So it can be, but there are times when it is more important to retain a card of exit.

Here is a hand on which the declarer went down to defeat in spite of a combined count of 28 high-card points.

```
            ♠ 10 8 2
            ♡ 7 4
            ◇ K Q 9 3
            ♣ K 7 6 2
                  N
             W         E
                  S
            ♠ A 9 4
            ♡ A Q 10 3
            ◇ A 6 5
            ♣ A Q 8
```

Both Vulnerable
Dealer South

SOUTH	WEST	NORTH	EAST
2 NT	Pass	3 NT	Pass
Pass	Pass		

West led the six of spades and East played the queen. Counting his winners in approved fashion, South saw that he had three tricks in each of the minors plus the major suit aces. A 3-3 break in either of the minors would provide his ninth trick and if all else failed he could fall back on the heart finesse.

Having learned how to hold up his aces, South played low to the first trick and low again on the spade continuation. His ace of spades won the third round as East discarded a heart, and he tested each minor in turn. Unlucky! Neither suit broke, and when South eventually tried the heart finesse West produced the king and cashed two more spades to put the contract one down.

The complete deal:

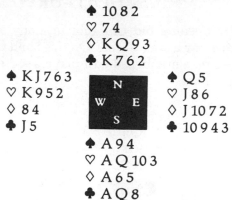

```
                    ♠ 10 8 2
                    ♡ 7 4
                    ◊ K Q 9 3
                    ♣ K 7 6 2
♠ K J 7 6 3          N          ♠ Q 5
♡ K 9 5 2       W       E       ♡ J 8 6
◊ 8 4                S          ◊ J 10 7 2
♣ J 5                          ♣ 10 9 4 3
                    ♠ A 9 4
                    ♡ A Q 10 3
                    ◊ A 6 5
                    ♣ A Q 8
```

South had apparently absorbed the technique of the hold-up without appreciating the reason for making the play. There is no point in holding up an ace when the critical finesse has to be taken into the dangerous hand.

Taking nine tricks is a simple matter on this hand. It does no harm to hold up once when the spades are attacked, but South should take his ace on the second round in order to keep an exit card in the suit. This makes all the difference in the end-game. South tests the clubs and the diamonds but West shows out on the third round of each, discarding hearts. It is clear that West has three spades and two hearts left, and South makes certain of the contract by exiting with his third spade. After scoring three spades West must return a heart, allowing South to make the ace and the queen.

MAXIM. Don't leave yourself without exit cards in the end-game.

---

80. GUIDING THE LEAD

An aggressive opening bid can gain in many ways, one of which is by indicating a sound lead. On this hand from a World Pairs Championship a number of East players soon had cause to regret their initial pass.

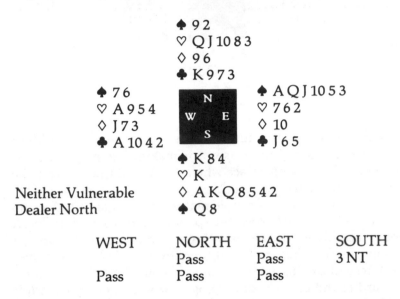

```
                    ♠ 9 2
                    ♡ Q J 10 8 3
                    ◊ 9 6
                    ♣ K 9 7 3
    ♠ 7 6            N          ♠ A Q J 10 5 3
    ♡ A 9 5 4    W       E      ♡ 7 6 2
    ◊ J 7 3          S          ◊ 10
    ♣ A 10 4 2                  ♣ J 6 5
                    ♠ K 8 4
                    ♡ K
    Neither Vulnerable  ◊ A K Q 8 5 4 2
    Dealer North    ♣ Q 8
```

WEST	NORTH	EAST	SOUTH
	Pass	Pass	3 NT
Pass	Pass	Pass	

When the bidding began with two passes, the South players opened with a bid of three notrump and played there. In the absence of any guidance from East, it was natural for West to lead one of his aces in order to have a look at dummy. The declarers then make nine or ten tricks depending on whether West found the spade switch or not.

At other tables East opened with a weak two spades, or even with a shaded three-bid. South still landed in three notrump, but the defense got off to a better start with a spade lead. Some declarers made nine tricks in spite of the spade lead, for the defenders needed to tread a narrow path to defeat the contract.

On the initial spade lead East plays the ten, and the declarer has to hold off to give himself a chance. East then has to find the switch to a low club, West putting in the ten when South plays low. The defenders thus made two clubs, two spades and the ace of hearts to put the contract one down.

This defense was worth most of the match points to those who found it.

MAXIM. Stretch to open the bidding when you have the chance to indicate a good lead.

---

81. SELF-INFLICTED WOUNDS

Declarers sometimes complain about bad distribution and diabolical defense when their troubles are really all of their own making. Here is a case in point.

```
            ♠ K
            ♡ 8 7 5 2
            ◊ K Q J 6 2
            ♣ K 8 5
```

```
                N
            W       E
                S
```

```
            ♠ A J 10 9 5 3
            ♡ ——
            ◊ A 5
            ♣ J 7 6 4 3
```

N-S Vulnerable
Dealer East

WEST	NORTH	EAST	SOUTH
		1 NT*	2♠
Pass	3◊	Pass	4♠
Pass	Pass	Pass	

* 12-14 HCP

West led the queen of hearts and North put down quite a suitable dummy. Ruffing the first trick, South played a spade to the king, returned to the ace of diamonds, and continued with the ace and jack of spades. West showed out on the third round and East, instead of continuing hearts as expected, played a second diamond, cutting the link with dummy.

Unhappy over this development, South continued with a third diamond. Both defenders followed suit and South discarded a club, but East ruffed the next diamond and South had to over-ruff. There was no real chance of finding the ace of clubs with West and the contract had to go two down.

The complete deal:

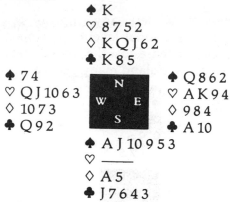

```
                    ♠ K
                    ♡ 8752
                    ◊ KQJ62
                    ♣ K85
  ♠ 74                            ♠ Q862
  ♡ QJ1063                        ♡ AK94
  ◊ 1073                          ◊ 984
  ♣ Q92                           ♣ A10
                    ♠ AJ10953
                    ♡ ——
                    ◊ A5
                    ♣ J7643
```

South ran up against a hot defense, for there are not many in the East seat who would seize the chance of breaking communications in diamonds. But South should not have exposed himself to this danger.

South can be fairly sure of scoring five trumps tricks and five diamonds. The trumps are likely to break 4-2, however, and after crossing to the king of spades South cannot afford to return to hand either with a heart ruff or with the ace of diamonds. The solution is not to strand himself in dummy in the first place.

Instead of playing a spade to the king, cash the ace to smother the king. It makes no difference to the trick-taking potential in trumps—just one trick has to be lost to the queen in any case — but it makes all the difference to the outcome. After forcing out the spade queen, South wins the return, draws the remaining trumps and claims his ten tricks.

MAXIM.   **Don't expose your communications to attack.**

---

82. THE ART OF BEING UNHELPFUL

Against aggressive bidders any slip in defense can be expensive, and at international level opponents are invariably aggressive. A careless defense cost the United States dearly in an Olympiad match against Poland many years ago.

```
              ♠ A 10 5 2
              ♡ J 8 6 5
              ◊ 9 6
              ♣ J 7 5
                          ♠ 9 8 6 3
                  N       ♡ A 10 7
N-S Vulnerable  W   E     ◊ A J 5
Dealer East       S       ♣ Q 6 2
```

WEST	NORTH	EAST	SOUTH
		Pass	1♠
Pass	2♠	Pass	3♡ *
Pass	4♠	Pass	Pass
Pass			

* short suit game try

West led the three of hearts to the ace, South following with the queen. How should East continue?

East continued with a heart, but this was not the right defense. South gratefully discarded a losing club and East won with the heart king, but the ace of diamonds proved to be the only other trick for the defense.

In the other room the final contract was the same, as was the play to the first trick, but the Polish defender found the unhelpful switch to a trump at trick two. There was then no way for the declarer to make more than nine tricks.

The complete deal:

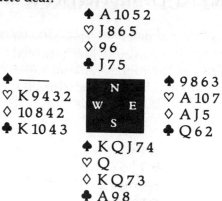

                    ♠ A 10 5 2
                    ♡ J 8 6 5
                    ◇ 9 6
                    ♣ J 7 5
♠ —   ♠ 9 8 6 3
♡ K 9 4 3 2   ♡ A 10 7
◇ 10 8 4 2   ◇ A J 5
♣ K 10 4 3   ♣ Q 6 2
                    ♠ K Q J 7 4
                    ♡ Q
                    ◇ K Q 7 3
                    ♣ A 9 8

Note that a diamond or a club return would also have allowed declarer to make his contract. It is only the passive trump return that is deadly. This is often the way when declarer has a lot of work to do in the side suits.

MAXIM. When declarer is in a tight contract beware of helping him out. Defend as passively as possible.

---

83. SUIT PREFERENCE

In leading to a trick a defender can often indicate by his choice of card the suit he would like returned, a high card showing preference for the higher-ranking side suit and a low card for the lower-ranking. On rare occasions it is even possible to indicate a trump entry, but a defender was inattentive on this hand from a tournament.

```
                    ♠ Q
                    ♡ Q 9 5
                    ◊ A K J 4
                    ♣ K 10 9 7 6
    ♠ 10 6 4 2        N          ♠ J 9 7 3
    ♡ A 6                        ♡ 7 4 3
    ◊ Q 9 3        W    E        ◊ 10 8 7 6 5
    ♣ A J 3 2         S          ♣ 5
                    ♠ A K 8 5
                    ♡ K J 10 8 2
Both Vulnerable     ◊ 2
Dealer South        ♣ Q 8 4
```

SOUTH	WEST	NORTH	EAST
1♡	Pass	2♣	Pass
2♡	Pass	3◊	Pass
3 NT	Pass	4♡	Pass
Pass	Pass		

Three notrump would have been completely safe, but South played in four hearts and West got the defense off to a best possible start when he led the ace of clubs and continued with the three. East ruffed the second club and hopefully returned a spade. The queen won, and declarer lost no time in discarding his remaining club on a top diamond. He then knocked out the ace of hearts and had no trouble in making his game.

East should have given a little more thought to his partner's choice of card at trick two. On the bidding South can hardly have four clubs, and it follows that the three cannot be West's highest card after the ace. Nor is it likely to be his lowest card since the two has not appeared.

If the three is recognized as a middle club, it must surely be read as a request for a trump return. A heart to the ace and a further club ruff is all that is needed to put the contract one down.

MAXIM.	Pay close attention to the spots in suit-preference situations.

84. PRE-EMPTIVE LESSON

One of the standard ways of making life difficult for the opponents is by the vigorous use of shut-out bids, and the basic rule when pre-empting is to go as high as you dare at the first opportunity. Lying low with a nine-card suit is unlikely to lead to a good result. See what happened on this hand from a Bermuda Bowl match between Brazil and Taiwan.

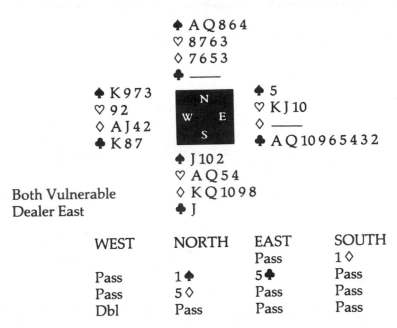

```
                    ♠ A Q 8 6 4
                    ♡ 8 7 6 3
                    ◇ 7 6 5 3
                    ♣ ——
    ♠ K 9 7 3                      ♠ 5
    ♡ 9 2          N               ♡ K J 10
    ◇ A J 4 2    W   E             ◇ ——
    ♣ K 8 7        S               ♣ A Q 10 9 6 5 4 3 2
                    ♠ J 10 2
                    ♡ A Q 5 4
                    ◇ K Q 10 9 8
                    ♣ J
```

Both Vulnerable
Dealer East

WEST	NORTH	EAST	SOUTH
		Pass	1 ◇
Pass	1 ♠	5 ♣	Pass
Pass	5 ◇	Pass	Pass
Dbl	Pass	Pass	Pass

The Brazilian East player decided to pass and await developments. He came in with five clubs on the second round but by then the opponents were able to judge that they had a cheap save. In practice five diamonds doubled proved to be a profitable enterprise for Taiwan.

West led the seven of clubs which was ruffed in dummy. A trump was played to the king and ace, and West switched to a heart. The declarer won, conceded a diamond to the jack, and won the next heart return. The jack of spades was covered by the king and ace, trumps were drawn, and the ten of spades was cashed. The marked spade finesse then permitted declarer to score three further spade tricks and dispose of his heart losers.

West could have defeated the contract by holding up his ace of diamonds and by keeping his king of spades to cover the ten on the second round. This destroys communications and prevents declarer from enjoying the fifth spade. Even if South plays a low diamond on the first round, careful defense by West can hold him to ten tricks.

But it is East who must carry the major share of the blame for this bad result. There was no need to give the opponents the chance to get together in the bidding. In the other room East for Taiwan opened five clubs and played there. On the natural lead of the king of diamonds eleven tricks were made for a swing of 16 I.M.P.

MAXIM.   When pre-empting, strike hard and strike first!

---

85. FREE CHOICE

South thought he was involved in a tricky question of probabilities on this hand, but his problem was really a simple one — he had a straight choice between making his contract and going down.

                        ♠ K 9 4 3
                        ♡ A 7 5
                        ◇ K 3
                        ♣ A Q 10 3

```
              N
          W       E
              S
```

                        ♠ A 10 7 6 2
                        ♡ K
Both Vulnerable   ◇ A Q J 6
Dealer South   ♣ J 7 4

SOUTH	WEST	NORTH	EAST
1♠	Pass	3♣	Pass
3◇	Pass	3♠	Pass
4 NT	Pass	5♡	Pass
6♠	Pass	Pass	Pass

The opening lead of the ten of hearts was won by the king and a low spade was played to the jack, king and five. South knew enough about 'free choice' to appreciate that the spade queen was likely to be with East. Holding Q J doubleton, West would have the choice of playing the queen or the jack. The fact that he has played the jack affords some presumption that the queen is with East. Furthermore, South held the view that this particular West, holding Q J doubleton, would have played the queen rather than the jack.

South therefore finessed in spades when East produced the eight on the second round. Unlucky! West had the queen after all, and a losing club finesse put paid to South's hopes.

The complete deal:

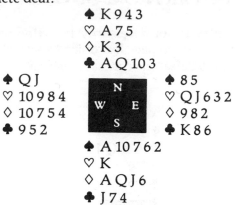

                    ♠ K 9 4 3
                    ♡ A 7 5
                    ◇ K 3
                    ♣ A Q 10 3
    ♠ Q J   ♠ 8 5
    ♡ 10 9 8 4   ♡ Q J 6 3 2
    ◇ 10 7 5 4   ◇ 9 8 2
    ♣ 9 5 2   ♣ K 8 6
                    ♠ A 10 7 6 2
                    ♡ K
                    ◇ A Q J 6
                    ♣ J 7 4

South gave himself the best chance in the trump suit but failed to see that he was rejecting a sure play for the slam. It really did not matter who had the queen of spades, for South can make certain of his contract by playing the ace on the second round.

As it happens the queen drops, but if West shows out South can continue with a diamond to the king, the ace of hearts for a club discard, a heart ruff and more diamonds. If East ruffs a diamond he has to return a club into the major tenace or concede a ruff and discard. It makes no difference if he refuses to ruff, for he is then thrown in with the queen of spades to make a fatal return.

MAXIM. Don't let the probabilities in a single suit blind you to the best play for the hand as a whole.

---

86. FAR FROM OBVIOUS

The obvious play is not necessarily the winning play at the bridge table. In defense, especially, doing what comes naturally is seldom enough to defeat the contract. Here is a case in point.

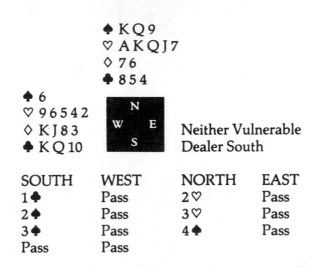

```
              ♠ K Q 9
              ♡ A K Q J 7
              ◊ 7 6
              ♣ 8 5 4
♠ 6
♡ 9 6 5 4 2        N
◊ K J 8 3      W       E      Neither Vulnerable
♣ K Q 10           S          Dealer South
```

SOUTH	WEST	NORTH	EAST
1♣	Pass	2♡	Pass
2♠	Pass	3♡	Pass
3♠	Pass	4♠	Pass
Pass	Pass		

The defense started well enough when West led the three of diamonds to his partner's ace. East returned a diamond to the queen and king, and West made the 'obvious' switch to the king of clubs.

What happened next was entirely predictable. South won the trick with the ace of clubs, drew trumps in four rounds, and chalked up his game with five trump tricks, four hearts and one club.

The complete deal:

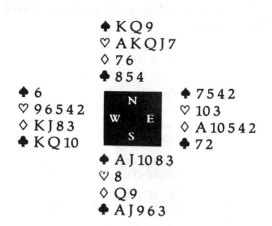

♠ K Q 9
♡ A K Q J 7
◊ 7 6
♣ 8 5 4

♠ 6
♡ 9 6 5 4 2
◊ K J 8 3
♣ K Q 10

♠ 7 5 4 2
♡ 10 3
◊ A 10 5 4 2
♣ 7 2

♠ A J 10 8 3
♡ 8
◊ Q 9
♣ A J 9 6 3

If West had given the matter a little more thought he might have seen that the club switch could hardly be effective. South was marked with five cards in each of the black suits and he was hardly likely to have a trump loser. West could count ten tricks for the declarer after a club switch, in fact.

Defensive hope stems from the fact that East is likely to have four trumps. In that case a heart switch at trick three may give declarer a headache by cutting the outside link with dummy. South wins and draws two rounds of trumps, ending on the table. Discovering the 4-1 break he switches back to hearts, but East ruffs the third round and South has to over-ruff. He returns to dummy in trumps and discards another club on the winning heart, but he has to concede two club tricks at the end.

MAXIM. Look beyond the 'obvious' in defense.

---

87. DANGER IS RELATIVE

In an attempt to avoid a trivial risk on the following hand the declarer exposed his contract to a more serious hazard which in fact proved to be fatal.

♠ A 7 6
♡ 8 3
◊ A K 10 9 5
♣ 7 4 3

♠ 10 5 2
♡ A K Q 6
◊ J 8 2
♣ A J 8

Neither Vulnerable
Dealer South

SOUTH	WEST	NORTH	EAST
1 NT	Pass	3 NT	Pass
Pass	Pass		

West led the three of spades and South reviewed the position. It looked as though West had led from a four-card suit but one could never be too sure about a defender's honesty. Just in case West was being clever with a five-card spade holding, South decided to hold up the ace of spades for one round. He planned to win the second spade, enter hand with a heart and run the eight of diamonds, making nine tricks even if the diamond finesse happened to be wrong.

South therefore played low from dummy on the first round of spades. East won with the king, but instead of returning a spade he switched to a low club. West won the trick with the nine and played the king of clubs to the ace. Naturally East had the queen of diamonds, and on regaining the lead he was able to cash two more clubs to put the contract one down.

The complete deal:

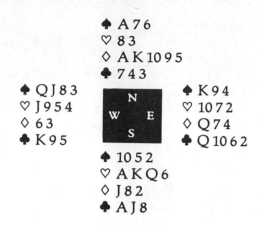

                    ♠ A 7 6
                    ♡ 8 3
                    ◊ A K 10 9 5
                    ♣ 7 4 3
    ♠ Q J 8 3   ♠ K 9 4
    ♡ J 9 5 4   N   ♡ 10 7 2
    ◊ 6 3   W   E   ◊ Q 7 4
    ♣ K 9 5   S   ♣ Q 10 6 2
                    ♠ 10 5 2
                    ♡ A K Q 6
                    ◊ J 8 2
                    ♣ A J 8

All one can say is that South was the victim of his own fears. It is true that West might have led a false card from a five-card suit, but this risk was miniscule compared with the risk actually run — that East would find a damaging switch to clubs after winning the first spade.

In general declarer should take his opponents' cards at their face value. After all, a defender does not normally try to mislead his partner. South should have won the first trick with the ace of spades, come to hand with a heart and finessed in diamonds. The defenders could then have won no more than one diamond and three spades.

MAXIM.   **Don't exchange a small risk for a big one.**

181

88. FELO DE SE

The bold buccaneers whose delight is to bid spades at every opportunity are fast vanishing from the bridge tables of the world. Nowadays most players realize that psychic bidding loses more often than it gains, but there are still a few die-hards with suicidal tendencies.

On this deal from a pairs tournament an ill-advised psychic bid showed the declarer how to make a slam that was booked for defeat.

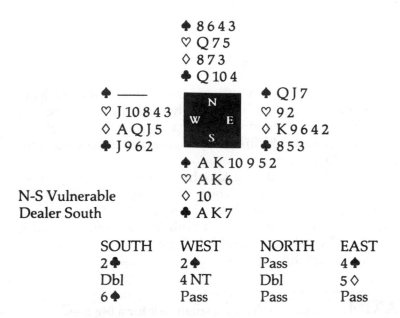

♠ 8 6 4 3
♡ Q 7 5
◊ 8 7 3
♣ Q 10 4

♠ ——
♡ J 10 8 4 3
◊ A Q J 5
♣ J 9 6 2

♠ Q J 7
♡ 9 2
◊ K 9 6 4 2
♣ 8 5 3

♠ A K 10 9 5 2
♡ A K 6
◊ 10
♣ A K 7

N-S Vulnerable
Dealer South

SOUTH	WEST	NORTH	EAST
2♣	2♠	Pass	4♠
Dbl	4 NT	Dbl	5◊
6♠	Pass	Pass	Pass

West intended to complicate the bidding for his opponents, but his psychic overcall of two spades had quite the opposite effect. When East raised to four spades it was not hard for the declarer to deduce where the outstanding spade honors lay. North's hand was limited by his first round pass and the double of four notrump showed his modest values well. This was all the help South needed to bid the slam.

Diamonds were led and continued, South ruffing the second round. After crossing to dummy with the queen of hearts, South returned a small spade and covered East's seven with the nine to make his slam.

At a number of other tables the slam was bid without interference. With nothing to warn them about the trump position, the declarers naturally cashed a high spade on the first round and went down to defeat.

MAXIM.   Avoid futile psyches.

---

89. LOOK, NO FINESSE!

Experienced players are familiar with a certain type of hand on which there is no need to take a trump finesse when the finesse is working. On such hands the declarer can give himself an extra·chance by trying to drop a singleton king. Here is a standard example.

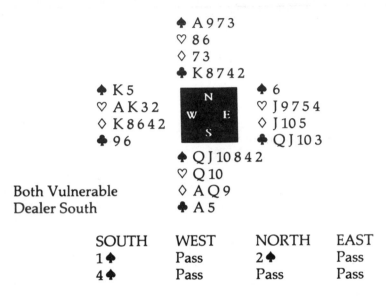

```
                    ♠ A 9 7 3
                    ♡ 8 6
                    ◇ 7 3
                    ♣ K 8 7 4 2
      ♠ K 5               N          ♠ 6
      ♡ A K 3 2                      ♡ J 9 7 5 4
      ◇ K 8 6 4 2    W     E         ◇ J 10 5
      ♣ 9 6               S          ♣ Q J 10 3
                    ♠ Q J 10 8 4 2
                    ♡ Q 10
Both Vulnerable     ◇ A Q 9
Dealer South        ♣ A 5
```

SOUTH	WEST	NORTH	EAST
1♠	Pass	2♠	Pass
4♠	Pass	Pass	Pass

West starts with the ace and king of hearts and then switches to the nine of clubs. South wins with the ace and tables the queen of spades, on which West plays the five. Should South finesse or not?

Looking at all four hands, you can see that the finesse works, but it is still a risky and highly unnecessary play. South should put up the ace of spades in an attempt to cater to a bare king in the East hand.

When the king fails to drop, South continues with the king of clubs and a club ruff. If West refuses to overruff he is thrown in with the king of spades and must return a diamond or a heart, either of which gives South his tenth trick.

Refusing the trump finesse loses only when West has all three trumps *and* the clubs fail to break 3-3 *and* the diamond finesse is wrong. That adds up to a 2% failure rate, and this is far outweighed by the 13% gain when East has the singleton king.

Refusing the finesse also gives an extra chance when East has the king and another trump, for the declarer cannot be forced to commit himself in diamonds before he knows if the clubs are breaking.

MAXIM. Always look for a way of avoiding a trump finesse.

90. DON'T SNATCH

Defenders often fail to appreciate fully the problems of the declarer and thus let him off the hook. On this hand a defender was in too much of a hurry to cash winners.

```
                    ♠ Q J 8
                    ♡ K 7 4 3
                    ◊ Q 8 3
                    ♣ K 10 5
        ♠ 6 4 3          N          ♠ 7 5
        ♡ Q J 10 6              ♡ A 9 8 5
        ◊ K 9 5    W        E    ◊ A 10 6 2
        ♣ 7 6 3          S          ♣ J 9 4
                    ♠ A K 10 9 2
                    ♡ 2
N-S Vulnerable      ◊ J 7 4
Dealer North        ♣ A Q 8 2
```

WEST	NORTH	EAST	SOUTH
	Pass	Pass	1♠
Pass	2 NT	Pass	3♣
Pass	3♠	Pass	4♠
Pass	Pass	Pass	

West led the queen of hearts to the king and ace, and East continued, as nine players out of ten would have done, with the five of hearts.

Seizing his chance, South ruffed with the spade ace, played the two of spades to dummy's eight, ruffed another heart with the king of spades, and played the nine of spades to the jack. After ruffing the fourth heart with his last spade, South crossed to the king of clubs and drew the remaining trump with the queen of spades, discarding a diamond from his hand. When the clubs broke evenly he had his ten tricks.

The defensive mistake was, of course, the heart continuation at trick two. This was unnecessary, for if the declarer had held another heart he could have no means of disposing of it. Looking at the cards on the table and remembering the bidding, East might have recognized the danger of helping the declarer to bring off a dummy reversal.

The safe defense is to switch to a passive trump at trick two. This leaves declarer with no way of making more than nine tricks.

MAXIM. Don't snatch at winners that can never disappear Defend passively and make declarer do his own work.

---

91. NO APPLAUSE

One feature that keeps the game of bridge alive is that good play is not always crowned by success. Nor is poor play invariably punished. The declarer fished for compliments after making his slam on the following hand, but none was forthcoming and, indeed, none was deserved.

♠ 6
♡ A 10 6 5
♢ Q 8 7 6 3 2
♣ J 5

```
        N
    W       E
        S
```

♠ ——
♡ K 9 8 4 2
♢ A K 4
♣ A Q 8 6 4

N-S Vulnerable
Dealer South

SOUTH	WEST	NORTH	EAST
1♡	Pass	4♡	4♠
5♣	5♠	Pass	Pass
6♡	Dbl	Pass	Pass
Pass			

West led the jack of diamonds against the doubled slam. South played low from dummy, East played the five and the king won. At trick two South played the king of hearts on which West played the three and East the jack. How should he continue?

The principle of free choice indicates that the jack is more likely to be a singleton than to be from doubleton Q J. Furthermore, the double seemed to suggest that West might have three trumps. When West followed with the seven on the second round of trumps, therefore, South finessed dummy's ten.

This worked out well because the complete deal was as follows:

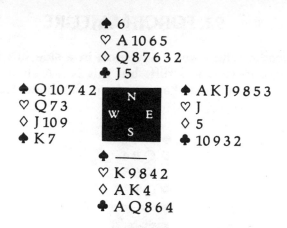

♠ 6
♡ A 10 6 5
♢ Q 8 7 6 3 2
♣ J 5

♠ Q 10 7 4 2   ♠ A K J 9 8 5 3
♡ Q 7 3   ♡ J
♢ J 10 9   ♢ 5
♣ K 7   ♣ 10 9 3 2

♠ —
♡ K 9 8 4 2
♢ A K 4
♣ A Q 8 6 4

Although the declarer's line of play was successful, it risked defeat if the trumps had been 2-2. When West follows to the second heart, the safe way to make the slam is to put up dummy's ace. East shows out, but South can ruff dummy's spade and continue with the ace and another diamond. If West is able to ruff he will be end-played, forced to lead a club or concede a ruff and discard. As it happens West follows to three rounds of diamonds and South can continue the suit, discarding clubs from his hand. If West refuses to ruff, he is eventually thrown in with his trump to make a fatal return.

MAXIM.   When faced with a choice of plays in the trump suit, look for the sure way of making the contract.

---

92. FORCE MAJEURE

A defender who owns a singleton in a side suit may feel a strong urge to try for a ruff, but this is not always the right defense. Look at what happened on this hand from a team game.

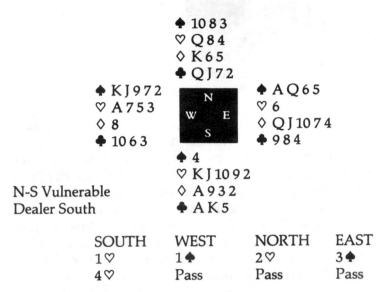

♠ 10 8 3
♡ Q 8 4
◇ K 6 5
♣ Q J 7 2

♠ K J 9 7 2
♡ A 7 5 3
◇ 8
♣ 10 6 3

♠ A Q 6 5
♡ 6
◇ Q J 10 7 4
♣ 9 8 4

♠ 4
♡ K J 10 9 2
◇ A 9 3 2
♣ A K 5

N-S Vulnerable
Dealer South

SOUTH	WEST	NORTH	EAST
1♡	1♠	2♡	3♠
4♡	Pass	Pass	Pass

The bidding was the same in both rooms, and one of the West players led the eight of diamonds aiming to score a ruff. This went to the ten and ace, and the declarer immediately tackled the trumps. West won the second round, put his partner on lead with the ace of spades and duly received his diamond ruff. That proved to be the last trick for the defense, however. On regaining the lead the declarer was able to draw the remaining trump and claim ten tricks by way of four trumps, two diamonds and four clubs.

In the other room West realized that his length and control in trumps indicated a forcing defense. He therefore started with a low spade. East won the ace of spades and returned the suit for declarer to ruff. The nine of hearts was allowed to win the next trick, and South continued with the ten of hearts. Now West had to be careful. It looks natural to win the second trump and continue the force with a second spade, but declarer has a neat counter to this defense. He discards a diamond from hand on the third spade, leaving the defense helpless. Dummy's queen of hearts can deal with a further spade lead and there is no way for the defenders to score more than three tricks.

West spotted the danger and held up his ace of hearts once more. This left declarer in real trouble. He could not afford to play a third trump, for West would win and force out his last trump with another spade lead. South was reduced to playing on clubs in the hope that West had four cards in the suit. When the clubs turned out to be 3-3, South cashed the ace of diamonds, played a second diamond to the king and continued with a third diamond, hoping to be allowed to ruff his fourth diamond on the table. However, West trumped his partner's winner on the third round of diamonds. Then he cashed the ace of hearts and forced once more in spades, leaving South with a losing diamond.

MAXIM.   Plan a forcing defense when you have length and control in trumps.

---

93. NO SWING

This hand from a match produced a bizarre result when one team played in four diamonds in both rooms. A big swing? Not a bit of it: the board was a push.

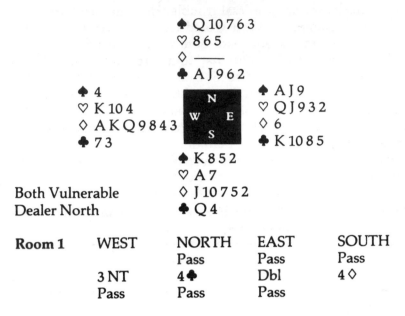

```
                    ♠ Q 10 7 6 3
                    ♡ 8 6 5
                    ◇ ——
                    ♣ A J 9 6 2
        ♠ 4                          ♠ A J 9
        ♡ K 10 4          N          ♡ Q J 9 3 2
        ◇ A K Q 9 8 4 3  W   E       ◇ 6
        ♣ 7 3             S          ♣ K 10 8 5
                    ♠ K 8 5 2
                    ♡ A 7
Both Vulnerable     ◇ J 10 7 5 2
Dealer North        ♣ Q 4
```

Room 1	WEST	NORTH	EAST	SOUTH
		Pass	Pass	Pass
	3 NT	4 ♣	Dbl	4 ◇
	Pass	Pass	Pass	

After three passes West opened with a gambling three notrump — a bid that might be thought out of place in fourth position. However, North contested with four clubs to show a major-minor two-suiter. This was a highly dangerous move at the vulnerability, although it might have worked out well since three notrump would probably have been made.

East doubled to show some strength and South temporized with a bid of four diamonds. When West passed North decided to wait for the double before rescuing, but the double never came. East chose to take the sure profit rather than risk driving the enemy into four spades. This was a good deicision, since four spades doubled would have brought in no more than 200 points.

Since his partner had doubled clubs, West led the seven of clubs and the king was allowed to score. East returned his trump, and South found himself held to three tricks for a loss of

700 points.

Room 2	WEST	NORTH	EAST	SOUTH
		Pass	1 ♡	Pass
	2 ◊	Dbl	Pass	2 ♠
	4 ◊	Pass	Pass	Dbl
	Pass	Pass	Pass	

East opened the bidding in this room and again North refused to be kept out of the auction. When the bid of four diamonds came round, South could have earned 11 IMP's for his team by passing. Indeed, he had no reason to do anything else, having only two sure defensive tricks opposite a partner who had passed originally.

However, South elected to double and the double-dummy defense of a heart lead proved too difficult to find. North led a spade to dummy's ace, and after a trump at trick two West made the same ten tricks that had been made in the other room. That was 710 to East-West — just another flat board.

MAXIM.   **Avoid dubious doubles.**

---

94. MISSED CHANCES

Bridge, like golf, is a game of misses. But while the golfer knows at once when he has played a poor shot, the bridge player may plod along for years without realizing that there is something wrong with his swing. Both sides made errors of timing on the following hand.

♠ A K J 10 3
♡ A K 9 5 3
♢ K 4
♣ 2

```
        N
    W       E
        S
```

♠ 9 7 5 2
♡ 7 4
♢ J 5 3 2
♣ 10 9 6

Neither Vulnerable
Dealer West

WEST	NORTH	EAST	SOUTH
1 ♢	Dbl	2 ♢	Pass
Pass	3 ♢	Pass	3 ♠
Pass	4 ♠	Pass	Pass
Pass			

West led the ten of hearts which was won in dummy with the ace. South cashed the two top spades hoping for an even break, but East discarded a club on the second round. South then reverted to hearts, cashing the king and ruffing the third round in hand. West over-ruffed with the queen of spades and played the ace and another club, but declarer ruffed in dummy, ruffed a fourth heart with his last trump, and led towards the king of diamonds, scoring ten tricks when West produced the ace.

The complete deal:

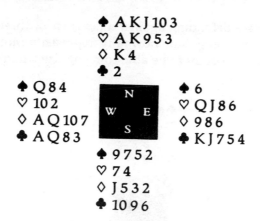

```
                ♠ A K J 10 3
                ♡ A K 9 5 3
                ◊ K 4
                ♣ 2
  ♠ Q 8 4            N            ♠ 6
  ♡ 10 2                          ♡ Q J 8 6
  ◊ A Q 10 7     W      E         ◊ 9 8 6
  ♣ A Q 8 3          S            ♣ K J 7 5 4
                ♠ 9 7 5 2
                ♡ 7 4
                ◊ J 5 3 2
                ♣ 10 9 6
```

Consider what happens if West defends a little more thought-fully, refusing to over-ruff on the third round of hearts. South needs to get back to dummy in order to ruff a fourth heart, but he has no quick entry. Whether he plays a club or a diamond, West can win and cash the queen of spades, leaving South with a loser in every suit.

It takes foresight to make sure of the contract after a heart lead. South should draw no more than one round of trumps and then play the singleton club from the table. This opens a line of communication between the two hands, and South cannot be prevented from scoring ten tricks.

Mind you, South will need to play with care if clubs are continued. After ruffing in dummy, he must cash the king of hearts and ruff a third heart in hand. If West refuses to over-ruff, South can play a diamond towards the king. When he regains the lead he can cash a second trump and ruff his last heart in hand.

MAXIM.   Look ahead and make sure of your communications.

---

95. DOUBTFUL ASSET

When you are defending against a contract of three notrump a stopper in an enemy suit normally represents money in the bank. But it is important to be able to recognize when the coin is counterfeit.

```
                    ♠ Q 9 7 4 3
                    ♡ J 10 8 3
                    ◊ 7 5
                    ♣ 8 2
                                    ♠ A K J 10 8
                         N          ♡ 7 5 2
Both Vulnerable     W         E     ◊ J 9 4 2
Dealer East              S          ♣ 4
```

WEST	NORTH	EAST	SOUTH
		Pass	2♣
Pass	2◊	Pass	3♣
Pass	3♠	Dbl	3 NT
Pass	Pass	Pass	

The opening lead of the six of spades was covered by the seven and won by the eight, South following with the two. The four of clubs was returned, and after a brief hesitation South won with the ace. South continued with three top diamonds and three top hearts, West following suit throughout.

For East the moment of truth came at trick three. The careless play of the two of diamonds would have enabled South to make his contract by means of a throw-in. But East realized that his diamond stopper was a liability rather than as asset. He played the four of diamonds under the ace and continued to unblock by throwing the nine and jack under the king and queen.

Here is the complete deal:

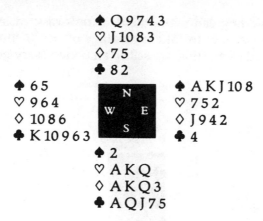

```
                    ♠ Q9743
                    ♡ J1083
                    ◇ 75
                    ♣ 82
    ♠ 65            N           ♠ AKJ108
    ♡ 964       W       E       ♡ 752
    ◇ 1086          S           ◇ J942
    ♣ K10963                    ♣ 4
                    ♠ 2
                    ♡ AKQ
                    ◇ AKQ3
                    ♣ AQJ75
```

You see what would have happened if East had kept any diamond except the two? He would have been thrown in and forced to yield a spade and a heart to dummy at the end.

As it was, the declarer scored an eighth trick with the three of diamonds but had no way of coming to a ninth. When West gained the lead with the king of clubs he shot back his spade to give East the rest of the tricks.

MAXIM.	**Unblock your high cards rather than submit to a throw-in.**

197

96. OUT FOR THE COUNT

Enemy bidding can make the declarer's task easier provided that he knows how to take advantage of it. On this hand the declarer erred by putting himself to an unnecessary guess.

```
            ♠ K 7 4
            ♡ A J 3
            ◇ 10 7 2
            ♣ A K 10 9
                 N
              W     E
                 S
            ♠ Q
            ♡ K Q 10 9 6 2
            ◇ A K 5
            ♣ 7 6 3
```

Neither Vulnerable
Dealer East

WEST	NORTH	EAST	SOUTH
		2♠ *	3♡
Pass	3♣	Pass	4◇
Pass	5♡	Pass	6♡
Pass	Pass	Pass	

*weak two-bid

North and South did well to reach the heart slam after the obstructive opening by East. West led the eight of spades to his partner's ace and East returned the jack of spades. South ruffed with the king of hearts, drew trumps in two rounds with the ace and the ten, and played off the ace and king of clubs, West contributing the queen on the second round. South discarded his third club on the king of spades, West following suit, and then played the ten of clubs from the table. When East followed low South ruffed, expecting to bring down the jack from West. Alas, West showed out and the slam was defeated.

The complete hand:

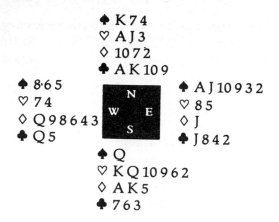

```
                    ♠ K 7 4
                    ♡ A J 3
                    ◊ 10 7 2
                    ♣ A K 10 9
  ♠ 8.6 5                              ♠ A J 10 9 3 2
  ♡ 7 4            N                   ♡ 8 5
  ◊ Q 9 8 6 4 3  W   E                 ◊ J
  ♣ Q 5            S                   ♣ J 8 4 2
                    ♠ Q
                    ♡ K Q 10 9 6 2
                    ◊ A K 5
                    ♣ 7 6 3
```

South claimed he was unlucky, pointing out that the clubs were more likely to be 3-3 than 4-2 in view of East's known spade length. This was true as far as it went, but there was no need to take chances on this hand. South could have discovered the exact truth about the distribution if he had thought to cash the ace and king of diamonds before tackling the clubs. After the play of the top diamonds, the top clubs and the king of spades, East would be marked with six spades, two hearts, only one diamond and therefore four clubs, and the winning play of finessing on the third round of clubs would have been a matter of routine.

Similarly, if East had followed to the second diamond, it would have been clear that he could have no more than three clubs.

MAXIM.   Don't guess at the distribution when you have a way of finding out.

---

97. STRUCK BY LIGHTNER

A convention that is frequently abused is the Lightner slam double which calls for an unusual lead — often a lead of the first suit bid by dummy. It is true that on borderline slam hands the opening leader may welcome his partner's guidance, but Lightner should not be employed without good reason. See what happened on this hand.

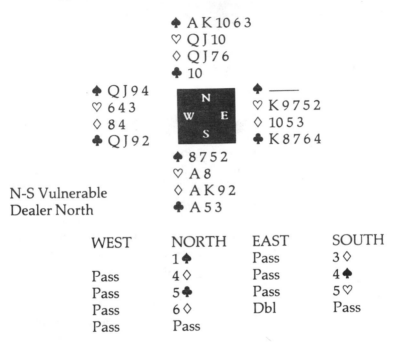

```
                    ♠ A K 10 6 3
                    ♡ Q J 10
                    ◇ Q J 7 6
                    ♣ 10
    ♠ Q J 9 4                      ♠ ——
    ♡ 6 4 3          N             ♡ K 9 7 5 2
    ◇ 8 4        W       E         ◇ 10 5 3
    ♣ Q J 9 2        S             ♣ K 8 7 6 4
                    ♠ 8 7 5 2
                    ♡ A 8
                    ◇ A K 9 2
                    ♣ A 5 3
```

N-S Vulnerable
Dealer North

WEST	NORTH	EAST	SOUTH
	1♠	Pass	3◇
Pass	4◇	Pass	4♠
Pass	5♣	Pass	5♡
Pass	6◇	Dbl	Pass
Pass	Pass		

West dutifully led the four of spades in response to his partner's double. However, it was clear to everyone at the table that East must be void in spades, and South therefore played the three of spades from dummy. East ruffed and returned a tricky nine of hearts, but nothing could save him at this point. South went up with the ace of hearts, drew trumps with the queen and king, and played another spade. When West split his honors, South won with the king, returned to hand with the ace of clubs and took a further spade finesse. The fifth spade provided a parking place for the losing heart, and a cross-ruff brought in twelve tricks.

The worst feature of the double was that it told the declarer how to make his contract. If East had kept silent, West might well have deduced the spade void from the bidding and might have produced the lead of a small spade on his own. In that event declarer would surely have played high from dummy and gone down to defeat.

A further point is that the double might have prompted either North or South to convert to six spades. All thirteen tricks can be made in spades with the aid of the heart finesse and the marked triple finesse in trumps.

MAXIM.   Double for a lead only when you are sure of defeating the contract and sure opponents have nowhere to run.

98. THE GOOD AND THE BETTER

The declarer was glad he knew something about percentages when a tricky decision had to be made in the play of this hand. But it turned out that he didn't know quite enough.

♠ J 10 5
♡ K J 8 3
♢ 7 6 5 4 2
♣ 7

♠ A K Q 9 7 2
♡ A 6 5
♢ A Q
♣ A 3

Both Vulnerable
Dealer South

SOUTH	WEST	NORTH	EAST
2♣	Pass	2♢	Pass
2♠	Pass	3♠	Pass
4♣	Pass	4♡	Pass
4♠	Pass	5♣	Pass
6♠	Pass	Pass	Pass

West led the queen of clubs, and when dummy went down South saw that he was in an excellent slam that depended at worst on finding one out of two finesses right. Trumps were drawn in two rounds, and South spotted a way of giving himself an extra chance in the heart suit. He played a heart to the king, returned a heart to the ace, and continued with a third heart towards the jack. This guaranteed him success not only when West had the heart queen but also when East had the queen singleton or doubleton.

In practice West showed out on the third round of hearts and South had to fall back on the diamond finesse. When that failed, so did the slam.

The complete deal:

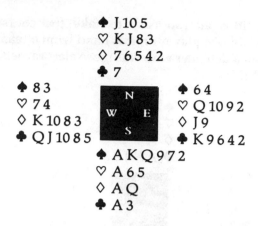

```
                    ♠ J 10 5
                    ♡ K J 8 3
                    ◇ 7 6 5 4 2
                    ♣ 7
    ♠ 8 3              N              ♠ 6 4
    ♡ 7 4         W       E          ♡ Q 10 9 2
    ◇ K 10 8 3                       ◇ J 9
    ♣ Q J 10 8 5        S            ♣ K 9 6 4 2
                    ♠ A K Q 9 7 2
                    ♡ A 6 5
                    ◇ A Q
                    ♣ A 3
```

South was certainly unlucky to find the hearts badly placed and the diamond finesse wrong. The total chance of success for his line of play came to almost 80%. And yet, better odds were available by tackling the red suits the other way round.

The right way to play the hand is to cash just one round of trumps and then play the ace and queen of diamonds. Success is certain if both defenders follow suit, for the fifth diamond in dummy can be established for a heart discard. And if someone shows out on the second diamond South can always fall back on the heart finesse.

Total chances for this line of play add up to more than 93%.

MAXIM. Having found a good line of play, look for a better one.

---

99. RISE AND SHINE

In defense it is all too easy to take the course of least resistance, as did one player on this hand from a team game. In the other room a defender who was more alert earned his team a swing of 10 IMP's.

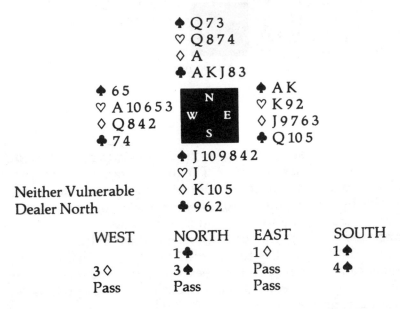

```
                    ♠ Q 7 3
                    ♡ Q 8 7 4
                    ◇ A
                    ♣ A K J 8 3
    ♠ 6 5                           ♠ A K
    ♡ A 10 6 5 3        N           ♡ K 9 2
    ◇ Q 8 4 2       W       E       ◇ J 9 7 6 3
    ♣ 7 4               S           ♣ Q 10 5
                    ♠ J 10 9 8 4 2
                    ♡ J
Neither Vulnerable  ◇ K 10 5
Dealer North        ♣ 9 6 2
```

WEST	NORTH	EAST	SOUTH
	1♣	1◇	1♠
3◇	3♣	Pass	4♠
Pass	Pass	Pass	

The bidding followed an identical course in each room, and the opening lead was the two of diamonds. Both declarers played a low heart from the table at trick two.

In one room East played low and the jack was captured by the ace. West switched to a club, won by dummy's ace, and another heart was led. At this stage it did not matter whether East played his king or not. Eventually the king was ruffed away and the queen of hearts provided a discard for the losing club. The declarer thus made his contract, losing only two trumps and one heart.

In the other room East realized that there could be no way of defeating the game unless his partner had the ace of hearts. He therefore went up with the heart king at trick two, cashed his trump winners, and exited with a second heart. Now the declarer was forced to fall back upon the club finesse, and when that failed so did the contract.

> **MAXIM.** Be ready to play 'second hand high' when necessary.

100. FIRST THINGS FIRST

It is easy to get the priorities mixed up when faced with a problem in card play. The declarer chose the wrong sequence of plays on this hand.

                    ♠ A 10 6 5 2
                    ♡ K 5
                    ◊ 7 2
                    ♣ A Q 6 2

                         N
                    W   E
                         S

                    ♠ K 9 4 3
                    ♡ 10 7 2
Neither Vulnerable ◊ A K Q 5
Dealer South   ♣ J 4

SOUTH	WEST	NORTH	EAST
1 NT*	Pass	2♡**	Pass
2♠	Pass	3♣	Pass
4♠	Pass	Pass	Pass

* 12-14 HCP
** Transfer to spades

West led the four of hearts to the king and ace. After cashing the jack of hearts, East continued with a third heart. West covered the ten with the queen and dummy ruffed. Now the declarer played a low spade to his king, wincing when West showed out. There was no way to avoid the loss of two trump tricks and the contract went one down.

The complete deal:

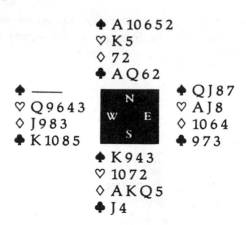

```
                    ♠ A 10 6 5 2
                    ♡ K 5
                    ◊ 7 2
                    ♣ A Q 6 2
    ♠ —                            ♠ Q J 8 7
    ♡ Q 9 6 4 3                    ♡ A J 8
    ◊ J 9 8 3                      ◊ 10 6 4
    ♣ K 10 8 5                     ♣ 9 7 3
                    ♠ K 9 4 3
                    ♡ 10 7 2
                    ◊ A K Q 5
                    ♣ J 4
```

South could have salvaged his game by finessing the nine of spades on the first round, but that would not really have been a sensible move. He might then have lost a trump trick unnecessarily, after which a losing club finesse would put the game beyond redemption.

The point is that on this sort of hand declarer cannot tell if he can afford a trump loser until he knows if he has a loser in the side suit. The first priority must therefore be to investigate the side suit.

After ruffing the third heart, South should play a diamond to hand and return a club for a finesse. When the finesse wins, he knows he can afford a trump loser and can make the safety play of a first-round trump finesse. If the club finesse had lost, South would have needed to bring in the trumps without loss and would start with a trump honor.

| MAXIM. | When unsure if you can afford to safety-play the trumps, test the side suits first. |

101. AVOIDING A GUESS

When an opponent has been active in the bidding, it is often possible to work out the distribution of the unseen hands and thus avoid a critical guess. On this hand the declarer did not give himself much of a chance.

```
              ♠ K 5
              ♡ J 7 6 3
              ◇ A J 7 6 2
              ♣ J 3
                 N
              W     E
                 S
              ♠ A Q J 10 9 8
              ♡ 4
              ◇ K 3
              ♣ A 10 7 2
```

Both Vulnerable
Dealer South

SOUTH	WEST	NORTH	EAST
1♠	Pass	2◇	2♡
4♠	Pass	Pass	Pass

West led the queen of hearts and switched promptly to a trump, thereby dashing declarer's hopes of ruffing a club on the table. South won in hand and played the two of clubs to the jack and king. Winning the trump return, he drew a third round on which West discarded a club.

East was marked with three trumps and presumably had six hearts for his vulnerable overcall, in which case he seemed likely to be short in diamonds. South pinned his faith on a second-round diamond finesse, but when East produced the queen the contract had to go two down.

208

The complete deal:

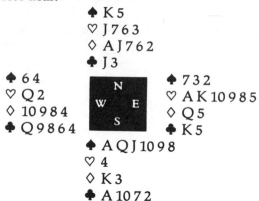

```
                    ♠ K 5
                    ♡ J 7 6 3
                    ◊ A J 7 6 2
                    ♣ J 3
     ♠ 6 4              N            ♠ 7 3 2
     ♡ Q 2                           ♡ A K 10 9 8 5
     ◊ 10 9 8 4    W        E        ◊ Q 5
     ♣ Q 9 8 6 4      S            ♣ K 5
                    ♠ A Q J 10 9 8
                    ♡ 4
                    ◊ K 3
                    ♣ A 10 7 2
```

Once declarer has placed East with three spades and six hearts he is almost home. After drawing trumps South should play another low club from hand. West would win and return the ten of diamonds to the two, five and king, and the play of the ace of clubs now brings the picture sharply into focus.

If East is able to follow suit, South would know that he had no more diamonds and would be able to take the finesse in complete safety. When in practice East discards a heart on the ace of clubs he is marked with two diamonds. Now the finesse is both dangerous and unnecessary. South simply plays off the rest of his trumps, forcing West to reduce to a singleton diamond in order to retain the queen of clubs. The diamond queen is now bound to fall under the ace no matter who holds it.

MAXIM. Count the hand to avoid guesswork in the critical suit.

THE BEST OF DEVYN PRESS
Newly Published Bridge Books

Bridge Conventions Complete
by Amalya Kearse
$17.95

An undated and expanded edition (over 800 pages) of the reference book no duplicate player can afford to be without. The reviews say it all:

"At last! A book with both use and appeal for expert or novice plus everybody in between. Every partnership will find material they will wish to add to their present system. Not only are all the conventions in use anywhere today clearly and aptly described, but Kearse criticizes various treatments regarding potential flaws and how they can be circumvented.

"Do yourself a favor and add this book to your shelf even if you don't enjoy most bridge books. This book is a treat as well as a classic."
—ACBL BULLETIN

"A must for duplicate fans, this is a comprehensive, well-written guide through the maze of systems and conventions. This should be particularly useful to those who don't want to be taken off guard by an unfamiliar convention, because previously it would have been necessary to amass several references to obtain all the information presented."
—BRIDGE WORLD MAGAZINE

Published January, 1984

Recommended for: all duplicate players

ISBN 0-910791-07-4 paperback

Test Your Play As Declarer, Volume 1
by Jeff Rubens and Paul Lukacs
$5.95

Any reader who studies this book carefully will certainly become much more adept at playing out a hand. There are 89 hands here, each emphasizing a particular point in declarer play. The solution to each problem explains how and why a declarer should handle his hands in a certain way. A reprint of the original.

Published December, 1983

Recommended for: intermediate through expert

ISBN 0-910791-12-0 paperback

Devyn Press Book of Partnership Understandings
by Mike Lawrence
$2.95

Stop bidding misunderstandings before they occur with this valuable guide. It covers all the significant points you should discuss with your partner, whether you are forming a new partnership or you have played together for years.

Published December, 1983

Recommended for: novice through expert

ISBN 0-910791-08-2 paperback

101 Bridge Maxims
by H. W. Kelsey
$7.95

The experience of a master player and writer condensed into 101 easy-to-understand adages. Each hand will help you remember these essential rules during the heat of battle.

Published December, 1983

Recommended for: bright beginner through advanced.

ISBN 0-910791-10-4 paperback

Play Bridge with Mike Lawrence
by Mike Lawrence
$9.95

Follow Mike through a 2-session matchpoint event at a regional tournament, and learn how to gather information from the auction, the play of the cards and the atmosphere at the table. When to go against the field, compete, make close doubles, and more.

Published December, 1983

Recommended for: bright beginner through expert.

ISBN 0-910791-09-0 paperback

Play These Hands With Me
by Terence Reese
$7.95

Studies 60 hands in minute detail. How to analyze your position and sum up information you have available, with a post-mortem reviewing main points.

Published December, 1983

Recommended for: intermediate through expert.

ISBN 0-910791-11-2 paperback

⟨Ꮲ THE BEST OF DEVYN PRESS
Bridge Books

A collection of the world's premier bridge authors have produced, for your enjoyment, this wide and impressive selection of books.

MATCHPOINTS
by Kit Woolsey
$9.95

The long-awaited second book by the author of the classic *Partnership Defense*. *Matchpoints* examines all of the crucial aspects of duplicate bridge. It is surprising, with the wealth of excellent books on bidding and play, how neglected matchpoint strategy has been—Kit has filled that gap forever with the best book ever written on the subject. The chapters include: general concepts, constructive bidding, competitive bidding, defensive bidding and the play.
Published October, 1982
Recommended for: intermediate through expert.
ISBN 0-910791-00-7 paperback

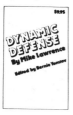

DYNAMIC DEFENSE
by Mike Lawrence
$9.95

One of the top authors of the '80's has produced a superior work in his latest effort. These unique hands offer you an over-the-shoulder look at how a World Champion reasons through the most difficult part of bridge. You will improve your technique as you sit at the table and attempt to find the winning sequence of plays. Each of the 65 problems is thoroughly explained and analyzed in the peerless Lawrence style.
Published October, 1982.
Recommended for: bright beginner through expert.
ISBN 0-910791-01-5 paperback

MODERN IDEAS IN BIDDING
by Dr. George Rosenkranz and Alan Truscott
$9.95

Mexico's top player combines with the bridge editor of the <u>New York Times</u> to produce a winner's guide to bidding theory. Constructive bidding, slams, pre-emptive bidding, competitive problems, overcalls and many other valuable concepts are covered in depth. Increase your accuracy with the proven methods which have won numerous National titles and have been adopted by a diverse group of champions.
Published October, 1982
Recommended for: intermediate through expert.
ISBN 0-910791-02-3 paperback

THE COMPLETE BOOK OF OPENING LEADS
by Easley Blackwood
$12.95

An impressive combination: the most famous name in bridge has compiled the most comprehensive book ever written on opening leads. Almost every situation imaginable is presented with a wealth of examples from world championship play. Learn to turn your wild guesses into intelligent thrusts at the enemy declarer by using all the available information. Chapters include when to lead long suits, dangerous opening leads, leads against slam contracts, doubling for a lead, when to lead partner's suit, and many others.
Published November, 1982.
Recommended for: beginner through advanced.
ISBN 0-910791-05-8 paperback

⟨ᑯᑭ⟩ THE BEST OF DEVYN PRESS
Bridge Books

A collection of the world's premier bridge authors have produced, for your enjoyment, this wide and impressive selection of books.

TEST YOUR PLAY AS DECLARER, VOLUME 2
by Jeff Rubens and Paul Lukacs
$5.95

Two celebrated authors have collaborated on 100 challenging and instructive problems which are sure to sharpen your play. Each hand emphasizes a different principle in how declarer should handle his cards. These difficult exercises will enable you to profit from your errors and enjoy learning at the same time.
Published October, 1982.
Recommended for: intermediate through expert.
ISBN 0-910791-03-1 paperback

TABLE TALK
by Jude Goodwin
$5.95

This collection of cartoons is a joy to behold. What Snoopy did for dogs and Garfield did for cats, Sue and her gang does for bridge players. If you want a realistic, humorous view of the clubs and tournaments you attend, this will brighten your day. You'll meet the novices, experts, obnoxious know-it-alls, bridge addicts and other characters who inhabit that fascinating subculture known as the bridge world.
Recommended for: all bridge players.
ISBN 0-910891-04-X paperback

THE CHAMPIONSHIP BRIDGE SERIES

In-depth discussions of the mostly widely used conventions...how to play them, when to use them and how to defend against them. The solution for those costly partnership misunderstandings. Each of these pamphlets is written by one of the world's top experts. **Recommended for: beginner through advanced.**
95 ¢ each, Any 12 for $9.95, All 24 for $17.90

VOLUME I [#1-12]
PUBLISHED 1980

1. Popular Conventions by Randy Baron
2. The Blackwood Convention by Easley Blackwood
3. The Stayman Convention by Paul Soloway
4. Jacoby Transfer Bids by Oswald Jacoby
5. Negative Doubles by Alvin Roth
6. Weak Two Bids by Howard Schenken
7. Defense Against Strong Club Openings by Kathy Wei
8. Killing Their No Trump by Ron Andersen
9. Splinter Bids by Andrew Bernstein
10. Michaels' Cue Bid by Mike Passell
11. The Unusual No Trump by Alvin Roth
12. Opening Leads by Robert Ewen

VOLUME II [#13-24]
PUBLISHED 1981

13. More Popular Conventions by Randy Baron
14. Major Suit Raises by Oswald Jacoby
15. Swiss Team Tactics by Carol & Tom Sanders
16. Match Point Tactics by Ron Andersen
17. Overcalls by Mike Lawrence
18. Balancing by Mike Lawrence
19. The Weak No Trump by Judi Radin
20. One No Trump Forcing by Alan Sontag
21. Flannery by William Flannery
22. Drury by Kerri Shuman
23. Doubles by Bobby Goldman
24. Opening Preempts by Bob Hamman

THE BEST OF DEVYN PRESS ♣

DEVYN PRESS BOOK OF BRIDGE PUZZLES #1, #2, and #3
by Alfred Sheinwold
$4.95 each

Each of the three books in this series is part of the most popular and entertaining collection of bridge problems ever written. They were originally titled "Pocket Books of Bridge Puzzles #1, #2, and #3." The 90 hands in each volume are practical and enjoyable—the kind that you attempt to solve every time you play. They also make perfect gifts for your friends, whether they are inexperienced novices or skilled masters.
Published January, 1981. Paperback
Recommended for: beginner through advanced.

TICKETS TO THE DEVIL
by Ricnard Powell $5.95

This is the most popular bridge novel ever written by the author of Woody Allen's "Bananas," "The Young Philadelphians," and Elvis Presley's "Follow That Dream."

Tickets has a cast of characters ranging from the Kings and Queens of tournament bridge down to the deuces. Among them are:

Ace McKinley, famous bridge columnist who needs a big win to restore his fading reputation.
Carole Clark, who lost a husband because she led a singleton king.
Bubba Worthington, young socialite who seeks the rank of Life Master to prove his virility.
The Dukes and the Ashcrafts, who have partnership troubles in bridge and in bed.
Tony Manuto, who plays for pay, and handles cards as if they were knives.

Powell shuffles these and many other players to deal out comedy, violence and drama in a perfect mixture.

Published 1979. . .Paperback
Recommended for: all bridge players.

PARTNERSHIP DEFENSE
by Kit Woolsey
$8.95

Kit's first book is unanimously considered THE classic defensive text so that you can learn the secrets of the experts. It contains a detailed discussion of attitude, count, and suit-preference signals; leads; matchpoints; defensive conventions; protecting partner; with quizzes and a unique partnership test at the end.

Alan Truscott, Bridge Editor, New York Times: The best new book to appear in 1980 seems certain to be "Partnership Defense in Bridge."

The author has surveyed a complex and vital field that has been largely neglected in the literature of the game. The player of moderate experience is sure to benefit from the wealth of examples and problems dealing with signaling and other matters relating to cooperation in defense.

And experts who feel they have nothing more to learn neglect this book at their peril: The final test of 20 problems has been presented to some of the country's best partnerships, and non has approached a maximum score.

Bridge World Magazine: As a practical guide for tournament players, no defensive book compares with Kit Woolsey's "Partnership Defense in Bridge" which is by far the best book of its kind that we have seen. As a technical work it is superb, and any good player who does not read it will be making one of his biggest errors of bridge judgment.

The author's theme is partnership cooperation. He believes there are many more points to be won through careful play, backed by relatively complete understandings, than through spectacular coups or even through choices among sensible conventions. We agree. If you don't, you will very likely change your mind (or at least modify the strength of your opinion) after reading what Woolsey has to say.

Published 1980. . .Paperback
Recommended for: Intermediate through expert.

DO YOU KNOW YOUR PARTNER? by Andy Bernstein and Randy Baron $1.95 A fun-filled quiz to allow you to really get to know your partner. Some questions concern bridge, some don't — only you can answer and only your partner can score it. An inexpensive way to laugh yourself to a better partnership.
Published 1979   paperback
Recommended for: all bridge players.

DEVYN PRESS
151 Thierman Lane
Louisville, KY 40207
(502) 895-1354

ORDER FORM

Number
Wanted

_____	101 BRIDGE MAXIMS, Kelsey. . . . . x $7.95 =	
_____	PLAY BRIDGE WITH MIKE LAWRENCE, Lawrence. . . . . . x 9.95 =	
_____	PARTNERSHIP UNDERSTANDINGS, Lawrence. . . . . x 2.95 =	
_____	BRIDGE CONVENTIONS COMPLETE, Kearse. . . . . x 17.95 =	
_____	PLAY THESE HANDS WITH ME, Reese. . . . . x 7.95 =	
_____	TEST YOUR PLAY AS DECLARER, VOL. 1, Rubens-Lukacs x 5.95 =	
_____	MATCHPOINTS, Woolsey. . . . . x 9.95 =	
_____	DYNAMIC DEFENSE, Lawrence . . . . x 9.95 =	
_____	MODERN IDEAS IN BIDDING, Rosenkranz-Truscott . . . . x 9.95 =	
_____	COMPLETE BOOK OF OPENING LEADS, Blackwood . . . . x 12.95 =	
_____	TEST YOUR PLAY AS DECLARER, VOLUME 2, Rubens-Lukacs . x 5.95 =	
_____	TABLE TALK, Goodwin . . . . x 5.95 =	
_____	PARTNERSHIP DEFENSE, Woolsey . . . . x 8.95 =	
_____	DEVYN PRESS BOOK OF BRIDGE PUZZLES #1, Sheinwold . . . . . x 4.95 =	
_____	DEVYN PRESS BOOK OF BRIDGE PUZZLES #2, Sheinwold . . . . . x 4.95 =	
_____	DEVYN PRESS BOOK OF BRIDGE PUZZLES #3, Sheinwold . . . . . x 4.95 =	
_____	INDIVIDUAL CHAMPIONSHIP BRIDGE SERIES (Please specify) x .95 =	
_____	TICKETS TO THE DEVIL, Powell . . . . x 5.95 =	
_____	DO YOU KNOW YOUR PARTNER?, Bernstein-Baron . . . . x 1.95 =	

*QUANTITY DISCOUNT
ON ABOVE ITEMS:
10% over $25, 20% over $50*

We accept checks, money
orders and VISA or MASTER
CARD. For charge card
orders, send your card number and expiration date.

SUB TOTAL [ ]

LESS QUANTITY DISCOUNT [ ]

TOTAL [ ]

_____	THE CHAMPIONSHIP BRIDGE SERIES VOLUME 1. . . . . x $9.95 (No further discount)	[ ]
_____	THE CHAMPIONSHIP BRIDGE SERIES VOLUME II . . . . x 9.95 (No further discount)	[ ]
_____	ALL 24 OF THE CHAMPIONSHIP BRIDGE SERIES . . . . x 17.90 (No further discount)	[ ]

ADD SHIPPING:
60¢ for 1 ITEM
$1.00 FOR 2 ITEMS OR MORE
SHIP TO:

TOTAL FOR BOOKS [ ]
SHIPPING ALLOWANCE [ ]
AMOUNT ENCLOSED [ ]

NAME _____

ADDRESS _____

CITY _____ STATE _____ ZIP _____